It's Not Your Journey
A Memoir

A raw and realistic look at my life with Bipolar
Disorder. Now that I am on this path, I might as
well try to help someone.

Rebecca Lombardo

Copyright Page

Printed in the United States of America

PubKick, 2015

ISBN **978-0692509739**

PubKick
PubKick@mail.com
www.PubKick.strikingly.com

In Loving Memory
Of
Barbara Jean Rounds
And
Dana Alan Rounds
Loving you and missing you every day.

"The semicolon represents the choice to continue life, because it is used when an author could have ended their sentence, but chose not to."

CONTENTS

Prologue
By Joe Lombardo

Teachers are amazing people and are found where you least expect it. Not just in school, but in life. One of the greatest teachers I've met in my life is my wife, Rebecca. From early on, when we first met, she starting teaching me. Unbeknownst to either of us. I've learned a lot from her. I've learned about love. True love, not the superficial stuff you see played out on television or movies.

I've learned about compassion, patience and doing everything in your power to support the person you love. I've learned about the ugliness of stigma and the pain surrounding those afflicted with mental illness. I'm a better person because Rebecca is in my life.

She's an amazing woman. I know that dutiful husbands often say that about their wives, but she truly is. She loves with her whole being, has an incredible sense of humor and only wants the best for her loved ones. She transcends her illnesses. She suffers from them, daily. They do not define her. She is more than just bipolar, depressed or borderline. She is a faithful wife. A loving daughter. A doting mother to our fur-babies. A steadfast friend to those willing to give her a chance and accept her for who she is, illnesses be damned.

She has bad days. We all do. Her bad days are usually much worse than what most people have to contend with. The incredible thing about this woman is the strength of her soul. She pushes on. Somehow, when others would've given up long ago, she picks herself up and keeps going. Admittedly, she has almost thrown in the towel a few times. Who can blame her? She is misunderstood quite often, even by her family.

This is where true love comes in. True love doesn't walk away when the person you love is falling apart. True love makes you the rock they need to support them in their time of need. It's a two-way street. Rebecca has been my rock over the last 14 years. I wouldn't have survived the passing of my father and grandmother without her. I would never have had the courage to change jobs without her support. I couldn't have handled the various ups and downs with my family and friends without knowing she had my back. She's my best friend and my partner in crime.

I hope you will read this book cover to cover. I'm confident you will gain a better understanding of how devastating mental illness can be. That you will learn to hold your judgment of those afflicted; replace that view with compassion and love. Perhaps, if you're dealing with these issues too, you'll find solace knowing that you aren't alone. No matter what, hopefully, my wife's words will teach you something, just as she has taught me over the years.

1

DAY ONE

NOVEMBER 13, 2013

This is my story. This book quite simply began as a blog. I used my writing as my own special brand of therapy in an effort to give myself some peace of mind. The more I wrote, the more people contacted me. They were grateful I came forward. Some have said that because of my bravery, they are finally able to understand how and why they need to get help. I don't consider myself the brave one. I believe the people that have taken my message and found a way to change their lives for the better, to be the heroes in this story. It may sound cliché, but just knowing that I have helped even one person follow a different path is all the fuel I need to keep writing my story.

There are many things that people don't know about me. Most of the time, they don't bother to hang around long enough to figure it all out. Often, there are those that know far too much, and it causes them to run for the hills. Regardless, I feel as if I finally need to give my feelings a voice.

What you may not know is that I suffer from Bipolar Disorder. The word "suffer" isn't to be taken lightly. I also deal with several other mental health related issues that we will tackle later. At the age of eighteen, I began to realize that something wasn't right. Now, at forty-one, you can imagine I've had many years of ups and downs. You want to believe after so many years life would be easier to navigate.

I'm sure people who've had no experience with mental health issues would find this to be the case. The truth is, you never know when it's going to knock you on your ass, or for how long. When the darkness creeps in, I'll reach out to someone. Usually, my husband, Joe. He understands my issues, having been there with me for the last thirteen years. I can always count on Joe to hold my hand through the storm.

My concern in writing this book is losing more friends and family members. It never ceases to amaze me how many people feel I am selfish or a freak. The stigma bug has bitten me before. My hope is in some small way my words will help people understand me a bit better. Perhaps they will learn to comprehend what the afflicted are dealing with as they make their way through life.

I'd love just to brush off the many misconceptions. Not care about what anyone else thinks. My flaws are many, but let's begin with being far too sensitive, caring about people who don't give a damn about me and possessing very little ability to deal with stress. Let's not forget I haven't the foggiest notion how to process grief. I face an arduous journey. Reliving these events will be painful. The next step is learning to deal with that pain, and whatever else might come my way.

2

THE YEAR FROM HELL

NOVEMBER 15, 2013

I have been debating for some time now whether or not exploring the events of the summer of 2013 will be healthy for me. I never anticipated that my behavior would alienate so many people in my life. I lost many friends due to my actions. Despite those losses, I can't let their ignorance determine my path to acceptance. The pain and resentment would eat me alive if I allowed it to.

It was an afternoon in late June. I can't remember the date. Ever since this incident, the Post Traumatic Stress Disorder (PTSD), which was once just a nuisance has escalated to short-term memory loss. Now, flashbacks, fear of the unknown, and consistent anxiety attacks plague me as well. There are incidents that I can recall quickly. Others, it takes a great deal of effort just to recollect a fraction of it.

I wasn't looking forward to turning forty, but I had no idea what was waiting for me once I hit that milestone. I started working for a direct sales company, which shall remain nameless. I was kicking ass, taking names, and loving it. I was winning sales awards, getting promotions, and meeting friendly people. Frankly, this aspect of the business world has eluded me, so I was proud of myself. Eventually, recruiting team members became comfortable.

My level of trust for them had grown to where I felt we could share personal details with one another. My depression symptoms were beginning to affect day-to-day life, so I went to them. I made them aware of what I suffered from, and the issues I was experiencing. It was a huge step for me. I received support and kind words, and it did help...for a little while.

One day, I found myself in a heated argument with my team. I can't even recall the topic. I will admit to my part in the dispute. Jumping to conclusions is my forte. However, I didn't deserve to be verbally insulted. Eventually, all of my team members deleted and blocked me from Facebook. It was painful, and it weighed on me. Phone calls began coming in from the company, reaming me out for allegedly mistreating my team members. It was simply not true. I did everything I could for them. Due to these circumstances, I became extremely frustrated, and flat-out told one of them she was a bitch. Big mistake. That caused a flood of more phone calls.

Some woman within the aforementioned company was calling me and acting as if I was a small child who had stolen another child's toy. I couldn't get a single word in about my side of the story or what these women did to me. Her only concern was the other women on my team. Finally, at my breaking point I screamed, "Leave me the hell alone!" and hung up.

It goes dark for me for a while at this point. I know I called Joe. I found myself in our basement collecting some sharp objects that I kept hidden down there. I recall sitting on the stairs and sobbing. I know that more phone calls and texts went out to Joe. For some time, lying on the floor of our office, I sobbed. Crying out to my mom, telling her I only wanted to be with her again. Why had she left me?

Lying on the floor in a patch of blood-soaked carpet, I heard the doorbell. It took me some time to get the strength to get up, and once at the door, I yelled,

"Who is it?!" It was my dad and my sister. My husband called them to watch over me until he could get home. Begging them to go away, they insisted they wanted to help. Knowing the next step would be 9-1-1, I had no other choice but to allow them into the house. There was an awkward silence. No one knew what to say at that point. I excused myself to my room to get some aspirin. Having a full bottle of an anti-depressant, I swallowed it all as if it were nothing, and casually strolled back downstairs.

I don't recall ever thinking to myself, "I want to die today." I merely wanted the pain to stop and to punish myself for all of the mistakes I made. Life had been going just fine until I screwed up, yet again. I meant to hurt myself, and if the result was death, that would be just fine. Everyone would be much better without me in their lives, right?

Joe came home and told me there was no way around it; we were going to the emergency room. Knowing now why this decision was necessary, I still can't help wishing he hadn't made it. Not for any other reason except the way things went once we arrived.

I spent several days in the hospital under suicide watch. There was always someone in my room, sitting in a chair watching over me. Interacting with those women was the only positive about the whole experience. They were kind to me when I needed it most. The doctors monitored my heart and liver to make sure I hadn't done any damage. Joe was there every day, and my dad came at one point. People said they would come but never did. Certain family members said that they couldn't see me in such a state. I felt hurt and abandoned by some of the most important people in my life.

After four days, the hospital came to us and said the state decided to have me committed. I was devastated. The EMT's came to get me. They wouldn't allow me to ride with Joe. They put me on a gurney and strapped me down. I felt like a fucking serial killer. I couldn't stop sobbing. They took me across town in an ambulance, which was about 110 degrees. Crying the entire trip, it felt like I was suffocating. My last ambulance ride had been to take my mom to the hospital when she passed away.

Joe was following us, which made me cry even more. I focused on his face through the back window, desperately trying to calm myself. The experience of being in that ambulance will haunt me until the day I die. When we arrived, they wouldn't let Joe inside. We were forced to say goodbye, not knowing when we would see each other again.

They strip-searched me. Literally. Bend over and cough, the whole nine yards. Patients were fighting in the hallway as the nurses filled out my paperwork. One patient received "the shot" and was left to drool in the corner of an empty room. I knew I had to play the game to get out of there as quickly as possible. We never received any help at all. Group therapy consisted of watching a movie or coloring. People threw feces out into the hallway or smeared it on their neighbor's door. The staff didn't give a damn about the patients and weren't afraid to say it. Even the cleaning crew swore at you.

I was there four days. It may not seem like a long time, but when you've been trapped in a nightmare, it feels like forever. My days consisted of doing word searches with a crayon. Occasionally, I wandered into the common areas. I couldn't stay long. The TV volume was so high it made my head pound. Patients were constantly screaming. They kept Jerry Springer on all day. Why they allowed it, I have no clue. I was living in an episode of the show. Complete with chair throwing and people fighting. Some chose just to yell at the walls.

Joe was allowed to visit on day three. They told me I was going home the next day. When he arrived to take me home, I was suddenly terrified of what to do next.

Walking out of that hellhole, I was aware my life would never be the same. It hurt to feel resentment towards Joe. He did what he felt he had to do. I realize how much pain it would have caused him, had I died that day. There will always be an ache in the pit of my stomach due to that experience. It feels like losing a huge chunk of your life you can never get back.

Some nights it feels like I'm back in that place. As if someone has walked into my bedroom to make sure I'm still in my bed. Now, looking back, I'm sure there is a reason for it all. I don't have an answer to that puzzle yet, but perhaps someday. I do regret my decision to hurt myself... to swallow those pills... to wish I wasn't here. Having seen the pain of saying goodbye without any answers, I do long to take it all back.

I'm telling my story not to gain attention, pity, or to make anyone feel bad. I need to get it out in the open where maybe it can help someone else choose a different way. I don't regret what I did because of where I ended up. I feel badly for all the pain I caused.

3

MY BIRTHDAY

NOVEMBER 19, 2013

March 23, 2011 should have been a happy day for me, at least on some level. It was my birthday, and having not yet turned forty, I was desperately clinging to my thirties. Joe was off work for the day, and we had plans to have an entertaining evening, or so we thought. Joe went out to run some errands, and I stayed at home, trying to relax. The phone rang, and from the caller ID, I knew it was coming from my dad's house. My assumption was that he was calling to wish me a happy birthday. When I answered, he didn't seem to be in a great mood, but my dad is a soft-spoken man.

He said, "It's Dana. He's dead."

Collapsing on the floor, all I could do was ask why, how, and what happened? Sobbing and barely able to breathe, I was unable to comprehend my brother was dead. My dad told me that he had gone to a friend's house that none of us knew and gotten drunk or high, possibly both. He got into this person's hot tub and drowned. He was brain dead by the time the hospital called my dad. The decision was made to take him off life support. I was never able to say goodbye. Looking back, I'm sure my dad thought he was sparing me in some way, but it's hard to see it that way.

I hung up, and called Joe immediately. I screamed into the phone, "Dana is dead, my brother is dead!" Joe rushed home, to find me sobbing uncontrollably. Dana was an alcoholic and had been my entire life. We all tried to help him. I even offered to go to AA with him. Eventually, we came to the realization that it was pointless to try because he had no desire to help himself. Every single day since his death, I find myself overwhelmed by a profound sense of guilt and loss.

He could have done so much with his life, had he ever stayed sober. He was so very talented and had a great sense of humor. He loved movies and music, and we shared CD's and DVD's regularly. He was the only person in my family that would call me if he heard I was sick or not doing well. I didn't appreciate those calls then, and I wish I had. Sometimes late at night, a call would come from my dad's house. It was probably my brother, and he was probably drunk. For this reason, we often didn't answer those calls. It was just too much to handle. Now I look back and wonder if perhaps I had taken more of those calls, would things be different.

I made a promise to my mom as she lay dying that I was going to take care of everyone. I was so obviously failing. I was angry with my brother before he died. We hadn't spoken since before Christmas. He was a no-show for our holiday dinners, and we never even received a thank you for the gifts we had sent.

Looking back on that day, I feel a profound sense of pain and anger. Did he do it on purpose? My dad has never been specific about the cause of death. He stifles his pain with his silence. I miss my brother. Every day.

He was a lost and angry man who couldn't come out of the depths of his despair. He couldn't fight the demons that kept him drunk, and I'm so sorry he's gone. If only we could go back to those last few months when we didn't speak. Perhaps things might have been different. I hope that there is a place called Heaven, and I hope my mom met him there.

He deserves to find peace, just once.

4

MISSING MOM

NOVEMBER 26, 2013

Today is November 26th, and it would have been my mom's eighty-first birthday, had she lived through the lung cancer and everything else. Her tiny little body may have been failing, but her mind was sharp, and she knew every horrible thing that was happening to her. I was there every single day, and I cared for her the best way I knew how. I went with her to radiation and helped her get dressed. I sat in the waiting room with the while the dumb ass soap opera played on the TV, praying each treatment would be the one that would wipe out the cancer.

Yes, my mom smoked, but at the time she was diagnosed it had been twenty-one years since she touched a cigarette. I was so proud of her for quitting but, unfortunately, we still had smokers in our house, and I'm sure that didn't help in the long run.

Those last few days she started to scare me. The radiation was making her throat hurt so badly that she couldn't eat or drink. They gave her a numbing medicine, but she said it didn't help. I talked her into going to the hospital, just to get an IV going and get some nutrition into her body, and we would come home.

My mom never left that hospital. I brought her there Thursday and on Saturday at 7:00 pm she was pronounced dead. I begged God to take me instead. To take anyone, just not my best friend, my confidante, and the one I turned to when things got rough. In the time since I got married and moved out we had become even closer, and I enjoyed talking to her every single day.

The lady who specialized in grief counseling came in and asked my dad if he had told her it was OK to let go. He hadn't, so Joe and I stood there as my dad leaned down to my mother's ear and said, "It's OK to go now. We've had a good life, and we all love you." I think that has to be one of the most painful things I have ever witnessed. My dad and I were in their living will, so he and I had to go out in the hall and talk to the doctors about whether we wanted her resuscitated should she go into cardiac arrest. The chances were high she would be worse off, broken ribs and all. We told them to take her off the ventilator and let her go.

I sat next to her for two days telling her things like how sorry I was that I was such a brat when I was a teenager, and I loved her so much. She was strapped down because she wanted to pull out the ventilator. I was able to hold her hand, and whenever I said I love you, she mouthed it back to me from behind the mask and squeezed my hand.

When she left us, I just fell to the chair and sobbed. The grief counselor asked me what I was feeling, and I just said, "I don't know what to do now." Since June, she had been my every day. She looked at me, and she said, "Make her proud." I remember that every day, in everything I do.

I wonder if she is or if she was. I think if she was here now and saw how far Joe and I have come she would be.

I just don't want to have to wonder and wish, I want her here. I miss my mom, and I want her back, if only for a little while. My mom wasn't a saint, she had negative qualities. Some people like to mention those negative qualities now that she is gone. It makes me want to kill them.

Then I remember that those people have ten times the negativity she had, and that is their lot in life, and they can live it. Don't enforce it on me. If I want to put my mom up on a pedestal and overlook her shortcomings, dammit I will. I loved her, and I love her still. How I wish I could be celebrating today instead of spending the whole day in tears.

Rest in peace, Mom. Always remember how much I love you.

5

ROLLER COASTER

I'm attempting to work through this myriad of emotions I'm feeling. It's hard for me to believe December is upon us once again. I'm sad, lonely, hopeless and hiding every bit of it. I know full well that when I start to hide the pain that I am feeling for whatever reason, things turn ugly. So, here I am. Broadcasting to the world that I am in pain, and I just want it to stop.

I remember a time when November hit, I couldn't contain my excitement. November meant Thanksgiving. Thanksgiving meant December, and December meant Christmas. Now, I lay awake at night dreading all of the above. When you lose important people in your life, things like the holidays are never the same again. I remember Thanksgiving 2007, my mom was declining fast, but still had her wit and her sense of humor. She was sitting in a chair in the dining room with her oxygen. She taught us how to make her famous stuffing balls before she had to start trying to make her way back upstairs to bed. She could take two or three steps and would have to stop and sit on the stairs for ten minutes. It was agonizing to watch.

We pulled it off. Thanksgiving went well, all things considered, and everyone enjoyed the dinner. My mom even made it down out of her room to eat with us at the table. She became tired quickly and needed to go upstairs, so I was helping her, and talking to her on the stairs. She finally looked at me and said, "I want you to know this will probably be my last Thanksgiving, and I am happy." Hearing those words was like a knife through my heart. We had to leave shortly after that because I didn't think I would be able to contain myself for much longer. The minute we got in the car, I lost it.

I kept saying, "Who says that to their daughter? Why would she ruin the whole night?" I cried and cried. I look back on it differently now. I was angry then because it was as if she was giving up and admitting that she was, in fact, going to die. I tried to believe otherwise no matter how she declined. Even her doctor had said that the radiation had made the tumor smaller. I held tightly onto that hope.

A few years removed from the Thanksgiving of 2007, I can look back on a lot of it and smile. She didn't eat much, but what she did eat she liked, and she would laugh from time to time and tell one of her jokes. She turned seventy-five on November twenty-sixth that year, and we spent part of her birthday at radiation. She once said that radiation was just a horrible procedure. She did it because she had to, and those people that called themselves doctors told us it was our only option. I would get her undressed and into her gown, and they would wheel her off. Without fail, every time, I held back tears.

They would bring her out, she would see me and her eyes would light up. I would smile and ask her how she was. She always said the same thing. "Fine." Once she admitted to me that seeing me sitting there waiting for her in the waiting room when she came out was how she got through it. She would see my face, and things weren't as bad.

As horrible of a situation as that was, and as hard as it was to take care of her every day, I always say that I wouldn't have it any other way. I don't want to feel guilt and pain because of her death.

I hope that someday I will stop blaming myself, and blame the damn cancer. Maybe not blame anyone or anything at all.

Wouldn't it be nice to have that sense of peace?

6

HOLIDAYS

I would hate to give anyone the impression that just because you are bipolar, you are constantly depressed. That is simply not the case. We have good days and even great days. What most people need to understand, however, is that the horrible days are multiplied by a thousand. A person who is bipolar may see your ordinary bad day as much worse than it is. We feel things deeper, and for longer periods of time. Yes, I do have good days, and there are times when my life brings me great joy. Unfortunately, the bad can outweigh the good by so much that you are just not sure you'll ever crawl out of it.

When I was a kid, Thanksgiving and Christmas meant everything to me, and my parents did their best to make sure we were all thrilled with our Christmas presents. Even if finances were tight, mom wanted everyone to have at least one present to open. Over the years, she kept that tradition alive. In my twenties, I still wanted to be the baby of the family, who got all of the cool stuff. When I got older, things changed for me. I started to feel more excited about giving than receiving, and I am proud of myself for that. These days, if I didn't get any gifts, I would be fine, as long as everyone else enjoys what I give them. Conversely, if they don't seem to enjoy it, it devastates me, so it's a double-edged sword.

Well, the last Christmas I remember having any enjoyment was 2007. Even though, my mom was sick, and she couldn't leave her room. My brother came home from South Carolina with his family. We hadn't seen them in years. We had a packed house, and I loved it. My mom and I had spent a couple hours a day on the computer ordering gifts for the family. Joe and I worked very hard on the food.

I went upstairs to check on mom every half hour or so. She seemed to be OK. It was obvious she was ill, but her mind was completely intact, and she was so thrilled to see everyone, even though she didn't even have the strength to get dressed.

It was the last Christmas we would all spend together, and the last Christmas we would spend with my mom. Her incompetent doctor at Beaumont Hospital had filled our heads with false hope, telling us that her tumor was shrinking. He told her not to worry about going back to another doctor for a while, just enjoy the holidays. My mom took that as, even if she wasn't doing well, she didn't have to go back to the doctor.

We lost her in January, so the holidays were never the same for me again.

I worked hard after she passed to keep her memory alive and follow along with some of her traditions. Even when Joe and I couldn't afford it, we made sure everyone had that one gift to open. We had all the dinners at our house because their house was too painful for me. Somehow, no matter how hard I tried, I always felt as if I wasn't doing enough. No one was appreciative, and I was heartbroken.

I kept that up for five years, even with the holidays bringing me nothing but pain and sorrow every year. We had become estranged from part of Joe's family. We had no one else to blame but me for that. No matter how hard I tried, they just didn't like me.

Nowadays, the holidays are more painful than ever. The members of my family that remain don't have the slightest idea how to communicate with one another. I am angry at someone almost daily, and for my sanity, I had to take a step back. I do not know how my mom did it every single year. I can't keep up her momentum that's for sure. After five years, I gave up. What did I get from that? Relief? Of course not. What I received instead was a healthy dose of guilt. That is what happens to a person with a bipolar brain.

I feel an overwhelming sense of guilt and failure if something doesn't go exactly as planned. And let's be honest, with my family, nothing ever does. I would get so excited about gift giving. I couldn't wait to watch them open the presents I had so carefully selected for them. Occasionally, they were well received, but many were just set aside with barely a thank you. It's not that I don't love my family. I do love them very much. I just don't feel like they see me for the person that I am. I think they all have serious misconceptions about me, and at this point in my life, I no longer care to try to improve our communication skills. I have many faults, and I know that. One of them is that I will hold a grudge. I will hold a grudge until you pry it from my cold, dead hands. I get that from my dad.

If you want the honest truth, I hate the holidays. It makes me sad that I do. Joe and I have tried to start traditions and enjoy ourselves, but nothing is the same. No matter how much time, money, or effort we put into everything, I always feel unappreciated. Doesn't anyone realize that it takes me ten times the effort just to put a smile on my face and move along?

I am so worried about what this Christmas is going to bring. Things haven't been going well with my family. I was too sick to go to Thanksgiving at my dad's house this year, and I can't ever remember a time that I didn't see them on Thanksgiving. Maybe I just wish I would have appreciated what I had while I had it.

Never take your loved ones for granted and always cherish your parents, even if they are different from you in every way. One day they won't be there anymore, and you will have to deal with the regret and sadness. I would love to get my family back together and celebrate like we used to.

Last year I even made a brief speech about putting it all behind us, and moving on. We are all we've got. I'm afraid it fell on deaf ears. Don't let this happen to you. Talk to your family. Do it before it's too late or and your relationships will become so toxic that you are terrified to be around them. What do I want for Christmas this year? A little piece of happiness. That's it. I don't need anything else.

7

COMING UP ON JANUARY

DECEMBER 23, 2013

For many of us, January is a time for a new beginning. We look forward to the New Year, setting new goals and hoping this one is better than the last. For some of us, the New Year brings pain, sadness, and regret. Perhaps, as in my case, January is just a painful month.

My Mom died in January of 2008. I hoped the pain would stop after a time. It's been years now, and it hasn't gotten any easier. I try to remember that she always wanted me to be successful and happy. It is one the most difficult times of the year for me.

By the time January rolls around, I feel like a heavy weight is pulling me down. I've stopped with New Year's Resolutions. I wanted to believe that they were a sign of hope and inspiration. The reality is I am putting far too much pressure on myself once again. Here is yet another huge list of impossible challenges that I can't possibly meet.

Perhaps this year, I will look back at the last year as a learning experience. Or, perhaps I can't shake the scars that it left upon me, physically and emotionally. I wish I could pause time. Try to find the spirit that I once possessed, especially at this time of year. 2014 has caused me a sense of panic. So, what do you do once you have spent three crippling months that have emotionally worn you down?

You grasp at anything that might bring you a sense of belonging. Of hope. You count your blessings that you are still here. You are grateful you learned from your mistakes. We all know that we could not have made it through 2013. We could have let the sadness and the helplessness become us, or change who we are. We did not. We are here and feeling so many emotions. That is OK. You are feeling something. I am feeling something. We won the battle. Now it's time to tackle the war.

Focus on what can be, not what has been. Try to let go of the past. I will if you will. I will not let my past mistakes define the rest of my life. If I make that mistake yet again in the New Year, then what is new about it? Rejoice in the fact that you can feel a sense of accomplishment at new, smaller goals. Goal #1?

Make it through January.

8

PTSD

DECEMBER 26, 2013

PTSD is just one of the many symptoms that I deal with on a daily basis. No, I haven't been in combat or seen anyone murdered per se, but that doesn't make the condition I have any easier to tolerate. Imagine that I am standing in the kitchen with my husband for twenty minutes. I can't see him, so when he taps me on the shoulder, I jump a hundred feet.

All night long I hear noises that sound like someone screaming or pounding on our front door. Sometimes when I am driving, I feel like the other cars are coming directly at me. So, you may wonder what a person does to cope with this type of anxiety.

I wish I could say that I have an excellent therapist that talks me through all of it. I do not. However, I do have Joe, and he is the next best thing.

The truth is that PTSD is a mental health condition that affects millions of people around the world and from all walks of life. Some may develop the condition due to the memory of a natural disaster, or a devastating event that rocks their community, for example a mass shooting. Others become chained by PTSD through personal traumatic events, the stress just eats them alive and can impact their everyday life.

About fifteen years ago, cutting was the only calming influence in my life. I was a pro. I had a box filled with about twenty different sharp objects. I even had certain songs that I played. I know from experience, there are many people that don't understand it. It helps if you think of it as a drug addiction. It calms you instantly. Then suddenly, just as fast as it takes the pain away, it gives it back to you three fold. Now not only do you hurt inside but you hurt on the outside too. Therein lies the vicious cycle of cutting.

Many of us do it to say, "Hello?!?! I am in pain here!" That is why I did it, and sometimes still do, as sad as that might be. The irony of a person like me is that I then cover it up because I don't want to look like a freak. So where does it end? It doesn't. Unless you make a decision that it has to. One of these days, the guilt is going to take over. You are going to start cutting and never stop.

I am proud to say that I am self-injury free since that horrible week in June 2013, and this time I plan on staying that way. I can't list off any particular coping mechanism that helps me in any way. I will tell you this, picture yourself locked away from the outside world and everything that you love. That will get you thinking just a bit clearer, believe me. I know I never want to end up there again. It's sad that something like this could still be an issue, but you have to remember that everyone has a burden that they carry with them. You may not be able to see it, but know it is there and try to find it within you to be kind.

9

EXPECTATIONS

DECEMBER 27, 2013

Expectations. We all have them. Some of us have higher expectations than others. I always thought I was sort of run of the mill. I didn't expect a lot for fear of disappointment. God only knows I have had my fair share of that. What I am so angry about is that at this stage in my life, I know I have to lower them more. I am going to have to stop letting people stomp all over my good intentions, and turn around, flip me the bird, and walk away.

You would think at my age that I could have found a happy medium. So why is it that every time somebody screws me over, hurts my feelings, ignores my feelings, or is just plain a complete douche, I still lose it.

I know for a fact I am a sensitive person that feels things deeper than a lot of people. The worst part of that is that the hurt lasts and lasts. It boils away inside of me until I just finally lose it.

When do I learn to stop letting people hurt me? I am not even talking about significant people in my life necessarily. People I barely even know find my weak spots somehow.

I think 2014 needs to bring out a lot of changes in my life. I don't want to become some cold hearted bitch who cares about no one, but let me tell you it's hard. Maybe getting my feelings out in the open will help me hurt less. One can only hope.

Expectations? Much lower.

10

THE BIPOLAR DEBACLE

DECEMBER 28, 2013

When I sit down and look back at all the ways suffering from bipolar disorder has affected my life, I just want to slam the closet door shut and walk away. It started as far back as I can remember. The old, "I have a headache and a stomach ache so, I don't have to go to school" got me through some of it. They weren't lies. I did honestly feel sick, I just didn't know why.

All throughout my high school years, it would come and go. A random teacher or coach would ask me if I was OK. Then, when I started to date, every break up hit me like a brick. We all think love lasts forever when we're fifteen. I invest every ounce of myself into a relationship. Should it fail for whatever reason, I take it as a personal assault on my character. Why wasn't I good enough? What did I do wrong? Is it because I'm fat?

I moved into my first apartment at age 19. I was working two jobs and going to school. Suddenly, I hit a wall. I couldn't function anymore. I suffered from severe insomnia so I would take ten or more Excedrin PM to go to sleep. When I couldn't stay awake, I took a handful of No-Doz. I hated me, and I hated my life.

Finally, I came to my parents and told them, and they helped me find a counselor; that worked for a little while. I was nineteen when I first started taking meds, and I still take them to this day. I've seen myself without them, and I don't like that person.

One painful side effect of bipolar disorder is trying to explain to people why you can't keep a job, can't stop crying, can't just snap out of it. Another is dating. I dated one guy who made a surprise visit to my parent's house. I invited him into my room to watch a movie. When he saw all of the pill bottles I had, he quickly exited. I never heard from him again. Good riddance to bad garbage.

I dated one guy very seriously through high school, and I thought he was "the one". Unfortunately, he was the **wrong** one. I spent a lot of years meeting people and trying to form healthy, lasting relationships, and it never happened. I even met someone online from New Mexico, and we were planning a wedding. Several months into the engagement, I had my first hospitalization for depression. He decided I wasn't worth his time anymore. He turned off his phone and pager and hung up on me if I called him at work.

I couldn't overcome the sadness and the anxiety. I had a stabbing pain in my chest. That is when self-injury became a big part of my life. It made it all stop for a little while. But it became my crutch. My only coping mechanism, if you can even call it that. Soon after I met an abusive jerk, that enjoyed making me feel unimportant, fat and ugly. I stopped eating altogether and lost a lot of weight. But, how much damage I did to my body, I will never know.

In 2001, someone came back into my life that made me feel like it was worth living again, and I married that man. Of course, we have good times and bad times. I still have highs and lows. He talks me through all of it. He is an amazing person.

It is possible. You can overcome all of the pain of your past and move forward, but it has to be on your own time. You can't let someone else dictate that you "ought to be feeling better by now". Nobody knows or understands, so you have to take care of yourself. If the medications aren't working, tell someone. If that person doesn't listen, tell someone else. But, remember you also have to do the work.

You can't strictly rely on the prescriptions because you could be stuck in that rut forever. Just try. Climb out of that hole a little bit more every day, and if you need me to, I will throw you a rope.

11

SELF ESTEEM

DECEMBER 29, 2013

When I was a kid, I was overweight, and a lot of people made fun of me. Hell, my last name was Rounds, who wouldn't jump on that bandwagon? When I look back now at how "fat" I was, I just wish I would have had one person in my life tell me that I was good enough just the way I was.

Instead, I cried all the time, starved myself and consistently abused laxatives into my late twenties. I love my family, but they were no help. Making fun of me, calling me names, and telling me to get my fat ass out of the fridge.

People, these tactics do **not** work. I have struggled with my weight and self-esteem for a staggering thirty years. And now that it has become a health concern for me, I think it's time to let the scared little kid inside of me go.

The simplest way to explain it is, self-worth comes just from where you think it does, yourself. You can marry the most supportive person in the world. You may have the greatest family and friends. When it comes down to it, if you don't feel good on the inside, none of that helps you believe in yourself.

Where does depression fall into this? Isn't it obvious? You eat because you are depressed. You gain weight because you ate. You hate yourself because you gained weight, and now you are overweight and depressed. Then it starts again. I know the pain of looking in the mirror and feeling worthless all too well.

Especially after you have been emotionally beaten down and made fun of most of your life. Add to that, practically everyone you know is thin and pretty and can wear whatever they want.

We all have our battle with self-esteem. Some don't like the way their hair looks while others don't like their nose. What we cannot do is let what some other small-minded person thinks of us change how we feel about ourselves.

Some people can change their perceived flaws, and some people can't. Regardless, I feel like we need to stop dreading the mirror and overcome the fear of being stared at in public. Stop looking at yourself in the glass doors at Target as you are walking in and stop beating yourself up over what you see.

Be you and be the best you that you can be. Try as hard as you can to be healthy! You will thank yourself years later when you finally stop letting the ignorance define you.

12

IS THIS A JOKE?

DECEMBER 30, 2013

Have you ever gone to the doctor, or even to the ER because you thought something was seriously wrong with you, and been completely disregarded? It happens to me on a regular basis. Thanks to my depression diagnosis, I am rarely taken seriously in anything I do. That is the vicious irony of the disease. It's too serious of a condition for you to be able to function normally. On the other hand, it's not severe enough to have any other aches or pains taken seriously.

I have gone to the ER before, and point blank told my husband, "Do not tell them about my depression." Why? Because whatever I feel is going on with me is met with that knowing, glazed over look in the doctor's eyes, as he nods and says, "Are you taking your medications?" Many people wonder why I don't go to the doctor, and I will give you three reasons right here and now.

Reason #1 I have been involuntarily committed three times after seeing a doctor.

Reason #2 I suffer from depression. Therefore, I am not taken seriously in any respect.

Reason #3 I am overweight, and according to every doctor I have ever seen, "You're just experiencing that because you're fat."

I can't decide which is worse. The blatant disregard for the seriousness of the reason I came in there, or the blatant disregard of the fact that I am a human being, and I have feelings. Wait, I'm fat? That must have just happened when I got here! I was a size two at home! Do they honestly think that this has never occurred to me? Do you know what I have been through in my life to try to change this?

Here's my favorite part of the story. The anti-depressants that I must take (believe me, if I don't, it's not pretty) are about 90% of the reason I am so overweight. So, now what Doc?

The medical profession is a joke. I used to have a healthy respect for doctors because I genuinely thought they were attempting to treat the person and not just a disease. I have found one doctor in the last twenty-five years that shows any kindness or consideration towards his patients. Even he isn't even right about what's going on a good portion of the time. Look, I am not asking for perfection here, I am just asking to be treated like I matter.

I suffer from depression, and I'm overweight. Those are just two of my characteristics, and they are not the only things that make up who I am. I learned a long time ago that you have to do the work to get better because you cannot rely on the medical field in any way. When you stumble or when you fall, you may be lucky enough to have a doctor there that will help you get back up. Try not to count on it. Keep calm, rely on yourself, and know that you are strong enough to make it through this, even if nobody else believes in you at that moment.

13

PROCESSING GRIEF

DECEMBER 31, 2013

When you lose someone in your life that is close to you, there's a part of you that dies as well. As I was entering my twenties, I knew that there would come a day when my parents weren't with me anymore. It still didn't seem real. It felt like if I just pushed that notion to the back of my mind, I could make it disappear. It isn't as if I had never had any friends or relatives pass before, but I think I shielded myself from the pain of it all. As crazy as it may be, the first death in my life that brought me physically to my knees, was my dog Boscoe. That was in 2005. My mom died in 2008. If I had known in 2005 that she had three more years to live, would I have called more? Come over more? Done anything differently?

I cried for weeks when Boscoe died. Suddenly, every

moment of every day I was talking to myself. "Oh my God, what if my Mom dies?" "Oh my God, what will I do when my Dad dies?" I became overcome with fear. In the past, death seemed distant, and I felt untouchable. Now, it was right here, present in my life, and I was terrified. I had persistent nightmares. My depression symptoms became much worse. Most days I was lucky to take a shower, and I could no longer work. My poor husband. Stuck by me through all of it. At one point, I had gone so long without leaving the house that on the day that I finally decided to try, the battery in my truck was dead.

I wouldn't allow myself to enjoy birthdays. It meant getting older. It meant getting closer to dying. I worried every minute about my parents...my husband. Why is he late? Death terrified me, and there was no escaping it. The idea of it consumed me.

In 2006, I began to feel like life was getting a little clearer. Like maybe things were going to work out OK for us. We bought our first house. Things were looking up. It was then that my mom started to get sick a lot. She always seemed to have the flu and trouble breathing. January of 2007, she felt ill, and I didn't know what to do. I didn't have a vehicle at that time, and I didn't think I could help.

It was June of 2007 when my dad called me from the car. He was rushing my mom to the hospital. She had a doctor's appointment and was having so much trouble breathing, they put her on oxygen and sent them straight to the ER. How did I not know it was this bad? Why didn't we get her help sooner? Dear God, please don't take her...that was all I could say. Please don't take her.

When I look back on losing my mom, and everyone else that has passed, it scares me how little I can cope with the grief. If I had one wish, it would be to learn how to deal with it effectively. I know I am always going to feel an overwhelming sense of grief due to those that I have lost and will lose. I just need to learn how to accept the fact that I am in pain, process it and get through it.

14

THERAPY?

JANUARY 1, 2014

Over the course of the many years that I have suffered from depression, I have met many doctors. For several years, I could only see a doctor in the county where I lived. I didn't have mental health coverage, and they would provide samples of the medications. It was a tremendous benefit in one respect because I could be on as many as seven prescriptions at a time. On the other hand, the level of care was substandard. Primarily, I was treated like a number on a file. However, without fail, whichever doctor's office I visited, my session ended with, what about therapy? Have you had therapy? Would you like a referral? My answer: yes, I have had therapy and no I do not want a recommendation.

I have documented my feelings on the medical

profession as a whole, focusing on the treatment of people with mental health issues. These feelings also extend to therapists. If you've never been to one but have seen one in a movie or on a TV show, don't even start believing that they are anything like that. I understand 100% that I have to do the work to get myself feeling better but damn! Shouldn't they have to do some work too?

Aside from that, regardless of how silly this may sound from a treatment aspect, I have not once ever felt better after a therapy session. I have always been the type of person who can work these things out on my own. I don't need to be paying someone who just stares at me with a blank expression on their face, barely listening. Perhaps, I have been to all of the wrong therapists. I'll go along with that. For over twenty years, every therapist I have gone to was completely useless but it was purely coincidental. Let's not forget the one I saw a few months back that fell asleep while I was talking.

I take my husband to all of my appointments due to the way Doctors and therapists treat me. That way, when I walk out thinking to myself OK, did that lady just fall asleep while I was talking to her? At least I have someone that was there who is not considered "mentally ill" that can back me up.

I know that I am only detailing negative experiences here, but they are my only frame of reference. I cannot, with a clear conscience say that all doctors and therapists are incompetent, and you will never find one that will help you. I know that is simply not true. Who knows, there is a common denominator here, and that would be me. Perhaps, without knowing, I go into these appointments immediately assuming they will fail. Therefore, it doesn't matter what is said or done, failure is the only outcome.

Now you can understand why this book is so important to me. Writing is my therapy. I may never receive an ounce of feedback on anything that I write, and that is OK because I have been allowed to tell my story. Without sitting in an office with someone staring back at me that so obviously couldn't give a damn about me.

Even if I do receive negative feedback from someone regarding my book, I can handle that because just as I am allowed to express my opinions here, others are allowed that same luxury.

If I do receive feedback that is especially hurtful or

bothersome, I will cross that path when I come to it. I am not sure how I will handle it. One thing is for certain; I am a stronger person for being able to document my experiences. In some cases, I receive praise for my writing ability or my courage in the face of all the pain I have and will endure. I will take it. I don't feel like there is a therapist out there that can offer that to me with any level of sincerity.

My suggestion is, don't take my words here and refuse treatment. That is the last thing I want for anyone. I want everyone to be aware of what can happen and what is out there. Do your research. Ask for a consultation to get to know the person first before you go about telling them your life story. It is true, you may have to pay for that appointment. Consider it paying for the peace of mind in knowing that this person is either a perfect fit or so far out of left field you will never be heard. Take someone with you. Someone you trust that knows at least part of the details of your situation, so that should you begin to forget details that person can help you fill in the blanks. Most of all, ask questions. Find out what a session will consist of, and how long they will last.

You can do this. Maybe someday I can do it too. I will know when I am ready, as will you. You will know when you have found the right professional to guide you as well. Remember, even if you feel like this person is a good fit, should their methods or the way they behave start to make you uncomfortable, do not go back. You are there to get better, and above all else, you should feel safe in that environment.

15

THE ANATOMY OF A PANIC ATTACK

JANUARY 3, 2014

Panic attacks. Most of us have had them, some more than others. All of the sudden, you have absolutely no control over your body or your emotions. I remember thinking recently about all of the crazy movies I have seen about people that are possessed and require an exorcism. I couldn't help but chuckle at the thought that perhaps I ought to give a priest a call.

In all actuality, there is nothing funny about a panic attack or the way you feel before, during, and after. Just the other day, I began to realize that my heart was beating faster for no apparent reason. Then came the pain in my chest and the loss of oxygen. I was breathing as if I had just jogged five miles. Then came the crashing wave of emotions. Fear, sadness, loss of control, and the sobbing. Sobbing so loud and heart-wrenching that it hurt my throat. The walls feel like they're closing in. Now what? I am here in the middle of this and I have no control over any part of me.

Stop. Think. Try to breathe. Call someone you trust. Write. Write down how you feel, what you were thinking of before it began, what you are thinking of now. Some people will tell you to go seek out one of your favorite things, like a TV show or movie. I know firsthand that this has helped me.

So, now you have made your way through it. The symptoms have, for the most part, subsided. Now you feel like you have been through a war. Physically and emotionally you are drained, and now is when you need to take care of yourself more than ever before. The worst part of "the after" for me, is the feelings of failure, or that I am losing my mind. We so desperately need to talk ourselves down from these emotions.

First of all, the fact that you are still here, and you made it through a very painful experience says that you are quite simply not a failure. Secondly, panic attacks do not mean you are losing your mind. You are scared, exhausted, and frustrated, but you are not losing your mind. One key point I would make to anyone who experiences these debilitating attacks, is don't seek solace on the internet or a message board. Imagine yourself in the middle of this situation, and you reach out to perfect strangers online, and you never get a response. Now you feel truly alone.

Find that one person that you can contact. Your mom, your significant other, your best friend, your therapist. Consider them your safe place. Even if they are just there on the other end of the phone listening, at least you are no longer alone. We all have it in us to use coping mechanisms to get through these situations, but we always need to remember that what may have worked a month ago, might not work this time around. That doesn't mean it will never work again; every situation is different. Try making a list one day when you are thinking more clearly. Write down things that you love to do or that you find comforting.

Most importantly, if you see a doctor for medication or even a therapist, tell them. Let them know these things are happening to you. Perhaps they will be able to offer you some advice. Try to stay open-minded. Especially when you are reaching out for a lifeline. Not everyone you know has had this experience, and many people are afraid of what they don't understand. This does not mean that you are in any way to blame for what is happening to you. Please, always try to keep that in mind. Coming from one person who suffers from depression to another, you should be proud of yourself for having made it this far. If you can try to keep that in mind, I will as well.

16

CHOICES

As far back as I can remember, we have always been fed the same philosophy about life. You grow up, go to college, meet the man (or woman) of your dreams, get married, move into a big house with a white picket fence, and have a whole gaggle of kids. That's what our parents did, or tried to do, so now it's our turn. What happens if life doesn't go that way for you? Have you failed at life?

In 2014, shouldn't we have advanced in our thinking, so that the moment two people get married, we don't instantly say, "So? When will you have kids?" I was lucky enough that my parents never said that to me, but I was honest from a very young age. I knew in my teens that I did not want to have children, but I was still told, "Oh, it's different when they are your own."

Sure, it's different. Just not for me.

The first time I ever went to a gynecologist in my teens, he told me that he suspected that I suffered from Endometriosis, and at that time you were told due to that you could not have kids. Then, this same doctor also told me that I was showing signs of cervical cancer. Well, here I am twenty years later, and I still don't have cancer, but I also don't have children. His diagnosis of Endometriosis was never verified, although it would explain a lot. I went on believing that it was the reason I went through such a horrible time every month.

Once I turned nineteen and was diagnosed with bipolar disorder, I felt as if I had finally been validated. I made the right choice in not dreaming of a house filled with kids. I could hardly take care of myself, who would ever think that I should attempt to care for a child? Now, the big question came in. Would there ever be a guy who wanted to marry the "crazy, psycho chick who also couldn't have kids"?

Let me be clear. I do not have documented medical evidence that my body cannot create a child. That possibility exists, so I am vigilant about making sure it doesn't happen. Mentally am I capable of creating a child? A thousand times no. Above all else, I would have to go off of my medications, and history has proven to me that doing that is a huge mistake that causes me and everyone around me a great deal of pain. Suppose the day comes that I have a psychotic episode, and here I am home alone with a baby? Or a panic attack, or just overwhelming sadness? Is it fair to subject a child to that? I think not. Is it fair to subject myself to that? Again, I think not.

After a long and painful journey through many failed relationships, I finally found a guy who loved the "crazy, psycho chick who also couldn't have kids". I have been grateful every day since I met him, because it takes a strong man to hold your hand when all you want to do is die. That is not an exaggeration; that is a fact. I know that he would have made an amazing father, and I do carry a sense of guilt for not being able to give that to him. He makes sure to tell me consistently that it wasn't only my decision, that he didn't feel that he wanted children either, so I didn't need to harbor that guilt.

When I established that being child-free was my only option, once again came the peanut gallery. Well, can't you adopt? No. I can't. What adoption agency is going to hand over a baby to a woman with four psychiatric hospitalizations? But, you can't really go about just telling anyone and everyone that little tidbit. So, I keep my fingers crossed that now that I have hit age forty, the questions will stop. Most people that know me well know that while I don't hate kids per se, I am also not especially comfortable around them. There have been a few that I have really enjoyed being around, but I enjoyed it even more when our visit ended. Not necessarily due to the children, but due to the level of anxiety I feel when they are around.

At a very early age, I suspected that children would not be in my future. However, it took a major diagnosis to make it "OK" to say I couldn't have them. Which, in my opinion, is a sad commentary on our times. Should you be of sound mind and body and decide that children are not your cup of tea, I feel as if you have just as much right to that option as people who want five kids, two dogs, two cars, and a summer home.

It's OK to decide that you don't want to have children, should you suffer from depression or not. If more people made that decision, perhaps we wouldn't have as many screwed up kids. That's just my opinion. And yes, I'm sticking to it.

17

ISOLATION

Do you ever find yourself stuck? Not really interested in seeing people or even just taking a quick trip to the store? Does it begin to feel like the only way you want to live? In all honesty, I would say that isolating myself is one of my biggest roadblocks. Especially this time of year, I find myself never leaving the house. I hate everything about January. The weather especially puts me in a bad mood, I feel like I am entitled to spend twenty-four hours a day, seven days a week inside my house. I keep telling myself that everyone will understand.

I let commitments slip away because I can't face the idea of leaving the house. I start to get down on myself and my appearance. I convince myself that once I lose a few pounds, it will be all right to see people again. It all feels very normal to me, and as long as I can wake up in the morning, and say to myself, "I don't have anywhere that I have to go today", I feel fine.

Suddenly, I realize that I have spent so much time alone that being around other people causes me a debilitating anxiety. I am terrified because I have taught myself that avoidance is best. Panic attacks set in, and I feel as if I can no longer cope. It's a vicious cycle. Once the fog clears a little, and you realize that you have been deliberately avoiding life for whatever reason, the guilt begins to kick in. Now you are more depressed than you were before.

Does any of this sound familiar? Have you heard from family or professionals that you are prone to this behavior, but set it aside thinking they don't know what they are talking about? You, my friend are isolating yourself. Just like me. Do I have all of the answers? No, of course not.

I do however have years of experience, yet I find myself walking down the same path, year after year. Anything feels better than anxiety. Even being completely alone. There are days when I long to be completely alone, but once I find myself in that position, I am so desperately depressed because I feel as if my illness is driving people away.

How do you find your way out of the dark? Baby steps. Quite literally. I start with showering and getting dressed. Possibly doing my hair and make-up. Once that mountain is conquered, I decide whether I have accomplished enough or do I feel strong enough to take on a little bit more?

Do I need anything from the drug store up the road? Maybe the car needs to be washed, or we need paper towels. However small the reason, if it gets you out of the house, even for half an hour, know that you have met your goal. Head on back home, knowing that you have succeeded for today, and perhaps tomorrow you can try again. Maybe stay out a little longer.

I often wait for my husband to come home, so that I can go out with him. Especially in the winter, when driving can be dangerous. If I am struggling, and begin to feel panicked, he can talk me through it. Find that one person who "gets" you. No matter who it is. Ask them if they will accompany you on a short trip. Do not let yourself back out. Have them meet you at your house.

Don't get me wrong, I don't want you to feel as if I am saying because you have isolated yourself, that you are now an awful person. I am not a terrible person, and I quite frankly succumb to the need to detach a few times a year. I just want you to find a way out of this hole you have crawled into. This behavior isn't healthy for any of us. You don't want to look back on life with regret. None of us wants to feel as if we have failed at anything. So, set yourself on a course for success.

It will be a struggle. Most things are when you are battling depression. The struggle is what makes you stronger. Feel proud of yourself for recognizing that you have this problem. I am happy that I have brought my isolation to light. If you can't do it today, especially due to the winter weather, make a <u>realistic</u> goal for yourself. I can tell you that when you return home from your errands, and you take a moment to think, you will feel a sense of relief. Now you know you can.

18

FAILURE

JANUARY 9, 2014

Ever since I was young, I had big dreams for myself. I mentioned before I knew in third grade that I wanted to be a writer. Eventually, I thought maybe I wanted to be a journalist, but taking ninth-grade journalism cured me of that idea. I was definitely not a "get in your face and ask the tough questions" person. I am a "stand in the corner and hope nobody notices me" person. It was OK though; I still had my writing skills, especially in creative writing. I would get published, and become a success.

When I got older, I knew something wasn't quite right. I cried far too much, and I was often sad for no reason. I lived in my fantasies. I wanted to be thin, I wanted to have a wonderful husband, and I wanted a great job. I shut out reality. I was going nowhere fast. I lost job after job for no good reason, and I often dreaded leaving the house.

Into my twenties, the only thing that helped me write was my sadness. My depression, now diagnosed, consumed me. I wasn't in school and I didn't have a boyfriend. I hated any job that I could keep for more than a month, and spent a lot of time online. This is when the notion set in that I had failed at life. I was a failure. I could see it on my parent's faces, every time I came home early after being let go from another job.

Why did I keep letting this happen? Yes, I suffer from depression, but is this the only life I can possibly lead? It felt like the word failure was written on my forehead. I carried it around with me everywhere I went. I never felt like I was enough. My self-esteem hit an all-time low, and I felt lost. Friends and family didn't understand. People were making a hasty exit from my life left and right. That was OK with me; I didn't want anyone to witness how badly I had screwed up.

May of 2001, my life completely changed. People will tell you that when you have found your place in the world, or found the great love of your life, you will know it. It's true, it really is. If you allow yourself to take down the walls you have put up around yourself, your whole view of life changes. Does it happen instantly? Nope. Do you automatically feel as if you have conquered your demons and you now lead a successful life? Nope.

Is there hope? Yes!

I often say that you can't just take the medications you have been prescribed and sit and wait for your depression to get better. You have to do the work too. I am not trying to sell you on the concept that if you think positive your life will all of a sudden live up to your expectations. Most of us try to think positive, and it doesn't help. This disease is far too strong for that. But, if you work at it, a little every day, and set small, realistic goals for yourself, you will start to feel that sense of accomplishment.

Are you in the same position as friends or people you went to school with? Probably not. Are they in your shoes? Most definitely not. So, why compare yourself to them? Maybe you didn't lose all of the weight you wanted to lose or get married before you turned whatever age, and you aren't the CEO of a Fortune 500 company.

What are you? A survivor. A warrior. You stood and looked your disease in the eye and said, no more!

I realize that now that I have turned forty, maybe I'm not as affluent as some people I know. Does it make me a failure? Nope. It makes me a success in a different way. I have quite literally been to hell and back, and I am still here...fighting. To anyone that is reading this that has looked back on their life and thought, "I have failed". Stop looking back. You can't change any of that.

What you can do is stay the course. Keep moving. Try as hard as you can to keep your head up. If you have a bad day, or a bad week, even a bad month, tell yourself that it's going to be OK.

You've made it through worse, you can make it through this. Stop comparing yourself to other people. This is something that I have been desperately trying to teach myself, so I know how hard it is. Believe me. If you ever want to feel a sense of normalcy again, you will learn from your past mistakes. Am I a failure? No. Are you a failure? No. Have we succeeded when we so badly had lost our way?

Yes. Be proud of yourself. You did it.

19

WHICH CAME FIRST?

JANUARY 13, 2014

We often hear people speak of the "chicken or the egg" theory. People often wonder, which came first? The same can be asked of which comes first in people that are both overweight and depressed. I know that I was overweight as a child. Was I depressed as I child? I don't necessarily think so, but I am both bipolar and overweight as an adult.

I have spent an entire lifetime struggling with my weight issues. Did I ever think that seeking treatment for my depression would contribute to that? Not in a million years. I don't blame the medications entirely, but I know that the worst of the weight gain started after I began taking certain prescriptions. If you research the side effects on most of them, weight gain is one of the first on the list.

Yet, I look back on all of these years dealing with this horrific disease, and I see where I went down the wrong path, and self-medicated with food. I often used food as a comfort for me in dark times.

My sophomore and junior years in high school were difficult for me. I had decided that I was fat, even though at that time I was just a bit overweight. That summer my parents allowed me to go away for a few weeks to a nearby college to join a program that offered journalism and other courses for teenagers. I decided that this was my first time away from the watchful eye of my parents, and I was going to take advantage of it. I was not going to eat. Not at all.

About four to five days in, I was too weak to attend all of the classes and the counselors started to notice. I finally went to the vending machine and bought a granola bar, and left it on my dresser. I was pondering whether I was going to eat it. I fell asleep, and ironically when I woke up, my roommate had eaten it. My first and only attempt at correcting my behavior, and it was gone.

After about eight or nine days there, I was going up the stairs on movie night and got to the top of the stairs and my shorts fell to my knees. I caught them just before I got to where about thirty people could see me. This should have been embarrassing for me, but I was on Cloud Nine. I made a lot of friends at that camp, and they realized what was happening and went to a counselor. She forced me to get into a phone booth and call my mom and tell her I wasn't eating.

A couple weeks later, I had been skating by with showing up for lunch and eating part of a salad, and that was it. When camp was over, and our parents were coming to get us, mine almost walked right past me because they didn't recognize me. I thought this was all great. I was apparently developing a dangerous eating disorder, but I didn't care. I finally felt like I was worth something being much thinner. Of course, when I got home I abused laxatives consistently because I couldn't keep up with not eating while my parents were around.

I gained the weight back and spent the next several years going back and forth between eating and not eating. Laxatives and no laxatives. Trying to throw up and consistently exercising. Sometimes in the middle of the night. What became of it all? I messed myself up so badly that now I could spend a month not eating, and I wouldn't lose a pound. I would probably gain weight.

Factor in anti-depressants that cause you to wake up in the middle of the night and cook yourself a meal, with no recollection of doing it. There were some mornings I would wake up with food in the bed with me. The medications had me so out of it that I was sleep eating. Now, I have gained too much weight, and I am almost forty years old.

So, looking back, I guess in my case, the depression came first. The low self-esteem and a negative body image caused the depression, which caused the eating disorders, which caused the need for medications. Now, it's all become a vicious cycle because my self-esteem is basically in the garbage from all of this weight gain. People will say, get off your butt and get in the gym. Yeah, I've done that. I've tried thousand dollar diet programs. Who knows how much I have spent on diet pills, and yes I have even gone back to old faithful, the laxatives. None of it sticks for very long because it doesn't work. Or the depression creeps back in, worse than ever before and weighs me down so that I can't even get out of the bed.

Every year, I swear this will be the year. I'm going to lose it. I have to lose it...one of these days I am going to find out that my health is in jeopardy. I know I have to get this done. Medical professionals can talk to me until they're blue in the face about how exercise is so good for depression, and endorphins...blah blah blah. That doesn't even cross your mind when it's a chore just to take a shower that day.

I know what I have to do. I have to stop believing that I will fail. I am never going to be super skinny, I know that. It's just not who I am. I just want to be healthy, and no longer in pain. Can I do it? Of course. Will I? I sure hope so.

20

STIGMA

JANUARY 28, 2014

Opening up about my life and what I have been through for well over twenty years, is one of the scariest things I have ever done. I had no idea what the reaction was going to be from friends and family. Did I really want them to know, and was I ready for the backlash? Once I came forward, I'm sure plenty of people thought, "Well, that explains that!" Those people don't concern me. It's the people that instantly judge based on little or no facts that trouble me.

The stigma that surrounds depression and anxiety is staggering. In my own personal experience, once someone finds out I am bipolar, I am rarely taken seriously again. People will be nice to your face, with a condescending smile, asking you how you are. All the while worrying you are going to flip out and kill them for even asking. That's my favorite part about this condition. You can't watch a true crime show anymore without discovering that the guy who killed eighty-seven people is bipolar. Let me tell you, it warms your heart.

People are almost always afraid of what they don't understand, and I get that. But, I'm still the same person. Depression isn't the only characteristic I have. I will probably always resent those people who walked out of my life at the darkest times. People don't always know what to say or do, so they just avoid you all together. That infuriates me. I'm the last person to turn my back on someone, and I at least expect that common courtesy from friends and family.

Sure, there are going to be times when I make plans with someone, and I can't follow through because my symptoms are just too debilitating that day. I may get angry or cry for some reason unbeknownst to anyone, but it's still me inside of here. I have a whole drawer full of medications, and I may jump to conclusions, be a control freak, and cry my eyes out all in about a ten minute time frame, but I am still here.

I still have feelings, especially when someone turns their back on me because of depression. Someone said of my recent hospitalization that I was selfish. I still laugh at the image of me sitting in a corner trying to hog all the depression to myself. As if it's a fun little novelty that allows me to have no control over my thoughts or emotions. It's a double-edged sword really. You want your disease to be taken seriously, because you never know when you might need real help. On the other hand, you don't want it taken so seriously that everyone you know puts you on his or her own personal little suicide watch. There's no happy medium for something like this. There's no happy anything.

You just have to deal with it, and hope that your friends and family will understand that it's going to be a bumpy ride. If they just keep their hands and arms inside the bus, they will get there in one piece. The advice I don't have? Where to find these people that will stick it out with you. I have an amazing husband that I adore, and a handful of friends that I can count on. Even if they don't understand what the hell is going on with me, they are there.

So, now that I have shared some of my deepest, darkest secrets with the public, how do I feel? The same actually. Maybe I feel a little better knowing I don't have to carry the entire burden around with me all the time.

I have to admit, it has been incredibly rewarding having total strangers reach out to me and say that my words have helped them understand their feelings, or my Facebook page helps them get through the day. It's gratifying, and it's one of the main reasons I decided to come forward. You have helped me just as much as I have helped you, if not more. For that, I thank you.

21

THE STRUGGLE TO COPE

FEBRUARY 7, 2014

I must have started writing this chapter a hundred times. There are many ways to approach this topic. Is it possibly too painful? Should I be safeguarding myself rather than bringing it to the forefront? I recognize that this must be dealt with carefully and with respect. I hope that once you have read this, you will feel that same way.

That is how people who cut themselves need to be treated, carefully and with respect. That isn't to say that you should become an advocate for the behavior. Just become an advocate for the person who carries that much pain and heartache.

I vaguely remember when it all started back in my early twenties. I had no idea that there was anyone else out there that did the same thing. I just knew I had to be insane. I didn't want to die, but I was in so much pain, and somehow self-injury relieved that pain for me, even if it was only for a brief period.

It becomes addicting. It's a vicious cycle. You cut yourself to express the pain the only way you can, but you hide the behavior from anyone that might actually be able to help. It had taken a couple of years before I was even able to go to my parents, and when I did they were so baffled and confused, they really had no words. We all just knew I needed help in a hurry. My body was covered in scars.

Self-injury really isn't the comical, circus freak way out of dealing with life that it has become to the general public. Some of my favorite TV shows make a mockery out of it, and even though at this time, I am "clean", it still gets to me. I just have to shake it off, but it hurts to be made fun of. Sometimes I will be at a store or a restaurant and I will see a teenage girl behind the cash register with scars on her arms, not that unlike my own. I feel for her wholeheartedly, and I wish I could take her aside and tell her what she is getting herself into.

If I had known anyone back when I started that had

been through this hell, and they could have spoken to me about it, maybe it would have made a difference, I don't know. What I do know is that the behavior that you think is helping you out of your anxiety, depression, or sadness is only hurting you and everyone that loves you.

When I think of the look in my husband's eyes when he has seen what I have done, it hurts me deeply. After having been hospitalized multiple times for such behavior, I know for a fact that it is not worth it. I needed to find effective coping skills for me as you should for any dark period in your life. Everyone will have different ways around it; some may seem silly and trivial, but I'll take that over self-injury any day.

I'm not perfect, there are still days where I have urges. However, I feel like I am better suited to deal with those urges. Not because of something a doctor said to me, or because one of my medications takes away the pain. Quite frankly, not cutting myself is truly the only answer. When I look back on the consequences of self-injury, that brief moment of time when I feel better just isn't worth the risk in the long run. Maybe it took this last hospitalization to realize it. The sheer horror of that whole experience has definitely left a lasting impact on my way of thinking.

One thing is clear. You must believe in yourself, and your ability to cope with whatever you are facing, and know that you are coming out on the other side a stronger person. Look back on your track record. You're still here, right? Maybe a little beaten down. Definitely a little bruised, but here. Nothing is going to change the fact that only the strong can survive what we have all had to endure. Remember that, and know that self-injury is never the answer.

There are many ways to fight the urge to cut yourself. Some of them might seem downright silly like, light a candle, turn on your favorite movie, read a book. Doesn't seem realistic, does it? How are those things going to help? You need to find what works best for you, and if one of those methods does work, that's fantastic! For me, the first thing I do is tell someone. I don't broadcast it to the world, but I walk up to my husband and I say, "Honey, I am having some serious urges to cut myself." You can't keep quiet about this issue or you won't be able to find a way out. Just saying those words out loud can calm some of the urges. If you aren't married, tell anyone that you can trust. It might scare them at first, don't take that personally. People are most often afraid of what they don't understand.

If you don't feel safe telling anyone, write about it. That may help you isolate the reason that you are having the urges and perhaps if it happens again, you'll know the signs and be better prepared. Having a journal is a valuable tool for any of us that deal with depression, anxiety and self-injury. Again, you need to find what works for you. It might even just start with a rubber band around your wrist. You snap it every time you feel the urge, and it gives you a certain comfort but doesn't scar you. Most of all, talk to your doctor, or your therapist if you do have one. You can do this. If I could go back in time and not have scarred my body in so many ways, I would do it in a heartbeat. I can't wear shorts or tank tops in the summer because of my scars. You don't want to end up like that. I promise you.

22

FEAR

FEBRUARY 25, 2014

We all have fears that can range from borderline silly to crippling and debilitating. The trouble is, that friend of yours that is terrified of cats doesn't see it as silly. Perhaps something happened in her life to change her beliefs or make her believe cats can hurt her. Is it our right to judge the seriousness of someone else's problems?

I have some very deep-rooted fears. I am afraid of heights, claustrophobic, and agoraphobic just to name a few. I am certain that there are people out there that find these fears silly. Go for it. Just remember to be perfect for the rest of your life.

These fears have become the cornerstone of my life at times. I get invited out, and I can't go. I may be faced with a harrowing ride in an elevator with far too many people in it. I have even had panic attacks watching people go into small spaces on TV. So it begs the questions, how do we fix it? Can we fix it?

The hardest part about fears is that the older you get, and the longer you go without addressing them, the worse they get. I have experienced months of isolation in my own home because of my fear of open spaces with too many people.

There are ways to cope. Obviously you need to talk to a professional about it, there's just no way around that. Take someone that you trust to the appointment with you as well. I never go to a doctor appointment without someone, because in my opinion, if you have someone there to back you up, they are ever so slightly less likely to tell you, "It's all in your head". Well, of course, it is. We're talking about **mental illness**.

It's a rather overused and stereotypical term, but all I can say is baby steps. For me, it started with being able to walk to the mailbox at the end of our driveway. I still kept my keys in my hand even though I unlocked all of the locks. Even writing it, and knowing I have been living it makes it appear silly. I understand why people just don't get it, I just wish they would try.

23

THE DARKNESS

Depression is a very deceptive disease. You could be having the time of your life on Tuesday, but come Wednesday morning, "the darkness" comes over you. Whom do you tell? What do you do? You were the life of the party last night, who is going to believe you that there is anything wrong with you today? Two weeks ago I began to experience "the darkness." I have come to a point in my life where I can actually feel my mood changing. It's just a certain feeling that comes over me, and I think to myself, "Here it comes. I'm about to crash". First thing I do is warn my husband. He needs to know that any mood swings or possibly confusing behavior is not due to something he has done.

So, it's here. What's next? Get out of bed? No. Take a shower? No. Get something done? No. Feel guilty about every single wrong thing you have ever done in your life? Check. Realize the house needs to be cleaned, and the dishes need to be done, so you are worthless? Check. The guilt hovers over me and takes control of my thoughts. I try very hard to tell myself that until this passes, the "to do" lists will have to be much smaller. Today, I will somehow take a shower. I have all day, right?

It's too much; I can't do that today. I just need to stay in this bed right now. I promise, I'll do it tomorrow. I am bargaining with my guilt. As a person who has gone through this for more than twenty years, I find it more and more difficult to reach out and say, today is a bad day, please help. I ought to be a pro, but I find that people begin to develop their own opinions and stereotypes as to why I am acting this way. "She is so selfish." "She is just trying to get attention." Or my favorite, "She's just lazy". Yes, please direct all of your attention this way. Let's tell everyone how I haven't left the house in weeks, and I can barely take a shower every four days. That's not humiliating at all.

We've all been taught coping mechanisms for situations such as this, but do they actually work? In my experience, there is a 50/50 shot that the coping mechanisms that we've been taught will help. I've heard it all before, but people just need to understand that there will be days in a depressed person's life that they cannot just snap out of it, or lighten up.

When the darkness does find its way into your life, brace yourself for what is to come, but try something new. Try to be optimistic. Don't obsess over how bad you are feeling. Whatever you do, don't try to make yourself an eight page to do list hoping that accomplishing it will make you feel better.

Just one task. That is all. As your mood starts to lift, make it two, and so on. Take a moment to stop and consider. Live in the moment and tell yourself, out loud if you have to, "I feel OK right now" or "I am so sad". These feelings are OK for you to experience.

If I leave you with nothing else this time around, let me leave you with this. It's going to be OK. It doesn't matter how long it takes, or what anyone has to say about you. It will be OK. One step at a time.

24

WHAT IS NORMAL?

When you suffer from depression, there is really no such thing as "normal" anymore. What you may consider to be normal, some people may not even be able to fathom. You wish you were ready to take on each day, and live it to the fullest. Most people wake up in the morning and go to work. They take care of their family and come home and have dinner. Most spend weekends enjoying their lives. Right? At this point, I'm not sure I am the one to ask. It's been a long time since I knew how any part of that felt.

For me, one of the worst parts about dealing with the symptoms is that I am well aware that there are people out there who just feel like I am lazy. Sometimes that thought even crosses my own mind. On those days when merely taking a shower is all I can muster, I beat myself up. I worry that more people will exit stage left out of my life. I fear my husband will finally begin to consider me a burden. Where would I go, what would I do if I didn't have him?

One of the hardest lessons I have to teach myself is that it doesn't matter what anyone else thinks or says. They are not living my life or dealing with this disease. I am constantly feeling as if I am being judged or mocked behind my back. Perhaps I am. I can't let that thought rent space inside my head. I just have to attempt to learn what normal is for me. At the same time, I have to understand that living under a cloud of sadness and depression cannot become my normal.

So, therein lies my struggle. Do I continue to beat myself up for not taking on more, or do I respect what I have been able to accomplish despite myself. Do I count my blessings for now? After all, I have succeeded in starting my own business, I have a lovely home, a wonderful husband. Perhaps I just need to let that be enough. Let me be enough.

There will always be a conflict inside of me. There will always be times such as this, where I can't find the light at the end of the tunnel. In the back of my head, I know I will come out of this but there is no telling when or how. One day I will wake up and not feel a sense of doom. I will have the energy and strength to begin my day, rather than roll over and cry myself back to sleep. I will stop letting fear organize my life.

As I become stronger and feel more capable of coping with life, I will look back on all of this pain and sadness. I will be grateful to have learned from the experience. I will come out on the other side a better person. That is my hope, and for now hope has to be enough.

I am alive and that for me, is my normal.

25

ONE DAY

Fear is a very strange thing. I deal with fear at the most nonsensical times. I'm not fortunate enough to be one of those people that has the strength to take charge of my fear and let it fuel me to do great things. I am paralyzed by the fear that grips my entire being. It's kind of funny that when I look back on my childhood and remember some of the days that I woke up terrified to go to school for some inexplicable reason, to get out of it, I always had a stomach ache. Which wasn't a lie, I did. It was just the anxiety taking over.

I don't know how this started. I don't think I will ever understand why it continues to happen to me today at forty-one years old. I always tell myself that you ought to have some insight into this by now. Thirty years of panic attacks, you would think I would be able to snap right out of it. And isn't that what everyone wants us to do? What we want to be able to do? Just snap out of it. What a glorious thing that would be.

At this stage in my life, I feel very, very tired. I am emotionally and physically beaten down by this disease. I don't know that anyone can ever truly understand the physical toll this condition takes on your body. Since I was nineteen, I have been to numerous doctors and on countless medications. Some would work for a short period of time, some none at all. I found bad doctors, and enough good ones to count on one hand. I've been hospitalized four times. Each time, I was barely able to focus on getting better because the conditions I was living in were so horrific.

So now, an average panic attack that ought to slowly subside, manifests into something even larger because I am perpetually afraid of that next hospitalization. Isn't that a sad and pathetic commentary on our times? You should be able to go to the hospital and get help, not stay awake all night because someone is stealing from you or your roommate screams her head off all night.

I know I am kind of bouncing around, and not really sticking to one topic. There is just so much to say, and I want to be able to say it before I forget again. On a day like today where for a brief moment, I caught myself and said...this moment is OK. I am OK, I just long for more of those.

I want to be able to wake up in the morning and feel eager to take on the day. Not afraid of what the day has to bring me. The ignorance of those that think I suffer from this condition on purpose is astounding. Be me for one day, I dare you. Until then, I will take a tiny bit of pleasure in the little things and try very hard to find the happiness that I know I deserve.

26

RELATIONSHIPS

APRIL 25, 2014

Relationships are difficult to navigate, especially when you suffer from depression. If you are one of the fortunate people, you've found a handful of people that understand your pain, your mood swings, and your sadness. You should consider yourself extremely lucky. I have spent most of my adult life terrified I was pushing people away, so I over compensated. When I was feeling healthy, I was too giving, offered too much of my time, and sometimes even my finances.

Eventually, if I hit a bad patch or wasn't able to be there for those people as I had been, they considered me too much of a burden, or selfish and no longer wanted to be friends. In the over twenty years that I have known of my illness, I have one friend who has always stuck by me. Unfortunately for me, she lives in another state. She has a very fulfilling life with a beautiful family, and I will admit I don't think to contact her during the dark times, because I know she is so busy. I don't want to feel resentment at having been "rejected" in a sense.

So, I lean on my husband. Perhaps too much. I am very grateful to have found him. I never have to worry that he won't be there. However, I still long for that bond with a girlfriend that I can chat with about anything, when things are good or bad. None of these relationships ever work out. I have been walked on, used, and treated like garbage. So, maybe I'm too defensive and too ready to confront the behaviors that bother me. I don't know, but the one thing I realize is that in all of these failed relationships, whether they are with friends or family, I am the common denominator.

It's a heavy burden to carry. The day you realize that is a difficult one. I struggle to convince myself that I am a decent person. I am just misunderstood. How can all of these people, most who don't even know each other suddenly decide that I am no longer worth the effort? I don't want to believe that I have to change. It's too overwhelming when you factor in the tribulations that I deal with daily.

The hardest part about all of this is that I just don't trust anyone anymore. I have always struggled with self-esteem, and if anyone paid me a compliment, I rolled my eyes and said, "Yeah right." Well, it seems as if the eye roll is back when it pertains to someone telling me that they care and are "there for me."

It's a hard lesson to learn that the only person that is ever truly there for you is you. Especially as you get older and the people you love begin to pass away, move away, or just become too busy to maintain a relationship.

The biggest irony in all of this is that people either love me or they hate me. There's never any gray area. There have been times when I know that I have deserved to be told off. I can own that, but I also know that there are times when I have not deserved it. I struggle with my resentment over those instances.

I think for now, I won't be concerned about popularity or creating friendships. I think I will guard what is left of my heart, love the people that matter and somehow find a way to like myself.

27

BODY IMAGE

MAY 13, 2014

When you suffer from depression, many things that might have been just a slight inconvenience in your life suddenly begin to define you. As a child, I was always a bit overweight. I was constantly bullied, sometimes even by my own family. The older I got, the worse it got, even though when I look back on those photos from those times, it occurs to me, I was absolutely not overweight. I would give a million dollars to be that "fat" now.

As time goes on and you're repeatedly subjected to name calling and abuse, the bad stuff starts to become easier to believe. If someone were to pay you a compliment, your standard response becomes, "Yeah right" and you walk away. My self-esteem was always in the gutter. Eventually, I had to shop in the "husky" department with my parents at Sears while all of my friends were wearing Guess or Esprit. The bullying got worse as people decided my eyes were too big, my forehead was too big, you name it.

By the age of eighteen, when the depression was really taking over my life, these were the only things I could think of when I looked in the mirror. I had long since been abusing laxatives and starving myself, and sometimes I actually lost weight. However, the damage I did to my body still affects me to this day.

Some of us who deal with depression let it take over our thoughts, and it teaches us to hate ourselves and our bodies. Which is why some of us resort to self-injury. I can remember not eating, taking laxatives, and doing sit ups incessantly. I studied every inch of my body. Believe me, I knew what self-loathing was at a very early age.

Now that I am older, I can't seem to get beyond those feelings. If you fast forward to now, you will see someone who is miserable, has no self-esteem and is overweight for many reasons. The primary reason, despite all of the other obstacles in my way, is that taking care of myself has always been too hard, too much of a burden. Don't get me wrong, I shower, do my hair and will at times wear makeup. I try to look nice for events and for my husband. But, what most people would consider just being lazy, I call depression.

One medication in particular that I take causes weight gain, and I've been on it over ten years. You do the math. Every day, I look in the mirror and I beat myself up. Why haven't you done this? Why didn't you do that? You swore you would lose this weight by the time you turned thirty-five, what is wrong with you?

Oh, if only it were that simple. Depression causes you physical pain, not just mental or emotional. When you are hurt or injured, many times the depression amplifies it so that you feel more intensely than the average person. This pain is what keeps me from doing whatever I can to exercise and get rid of some of this weight.

Now, I know there is just no way around it. I am miserable. I don't leave my house anymore. I don't want anyone to see me like this. One day, I hope to wake up and realize that every scar, every stretch mark, and every imperfection is what makes me beautiful. Every day I fight what most would consider a losing battle. Sometimes, I come out on top because I made it through.

When the time comes, and you are ready to maybe drop a few pounds, start an exercise program, and change your eating habits, you will have the confidence to succeed because you are a fighter.

Just try. As hard as it is, just try. I know it's easier just to lie in that bed and cry. I have resorted to that myself on many occasions. Please...for you, your family, and for me, just try. I'll be right there with you, trying as well. You can do this. You are not just a survivor; you are a warrior.

28

MOVING ON

MAY 25, 2014

Strength, for me, is fleeting. The confidence I may feel on any given day will most likely not be duplicated on the following day. Weakness, however, seems to be a constant. Each and every day there will be multiple occasions where I decide that I just can't do it anymore. I can't try, I can't fight, and I certainly can't win.

I can feel it as it comes on. It's almost as if someone comes along and drops a hundred pound weight on me. Thud. There it is. Wasn't I just washing the dishes? Didn't I just answer my emails? I vacuumed not twenty minutes ago, right? Gone. It's as if none of it ever happened. I can't even take comfort in the fact that I did accomplish these things because the weakness is so much bigger than any of that.

I know the old me still exists. I have to believe that or I will never get out of bed again. I strive every day, even for just a moment to find her. She seems lost forever. So, I beat myself up. I relive every second of every horrible thing that has happened to me in a flash.

One of the worst parts about it is the feelings of loss. I have a handful of people that I can trust or rely on, and that list gets smaller every day. Pretty soon the handful will become a thimble full, and then there will be none. Nobody knows better than I do how overwhelming it is to have someone who suffers from depression in your life. I have never once asked that anyone change or be forced to adapt to my life. I did however anticipate that, at the very least, my family would be there. I guess I need to let that go and move on.

If strength is gained from each and every painful lesson, I have nothing to worry about. I have absolutely no shortage of painful lessons. I suppose I just look in the mirror sometimes and have no clue who I am looking at. Don't allow yourself to get bogged down by the "should" or the "could". As someone once told me, you have to learn to forgive yourself sometimes.

Consider that depression does not equal weakness. Weakness is a side effect at times, but that doesn't mean that you <u>are</u> weakness. I know that it all seems so very overwhelming. That is where you have to come to the realization that you may not ever be the exact person that you once were, but perhaps you are a better, stronger version. You just have to be willing to let it happen. I have to be willing.

If today isn't the day, it's OK. Perhaps it will be tomorrow or the next day. Any of these are options, and a reason to carry on. Look back on the past from time to time, but don't get stuck there. Big mistake. Huge mistake. It takes a strong person to admit that.

29

LETTING GO

JUNE 18, 2014

Letting go can be one of the most difficult decisions you have to make in your life. Especially when it comes to people that you so desperately want to care about. Suddenly, you come to the realization that they don't care for you nearly on the level that you care for them. Now you find yourself systematically following through with the stages of grief.

For me, anger is the hardest stage to get through. When all you wanted was a thank you or a good job now and then, it's hard not to be angry. For years and years I let my own feelings fall by the wayside and only worried about everyone else. Look where I find myself now? Estranged from all of the people that should be the first ones to be by my side when the chips are down.

Now that all of the name-calling and the finger pointing is out of the way, I have decided that I am done. I will no longer place myself in unhealthy situations or toxic relationships, just because I am "supposed to". The people that have hurt me the most in life will continue their narrow-minded view of me, my life, and my illness. I can no longer allow that to dictate whether or not I find happiness in my life. I have to be stronger than that, and I have to be stronger than their opinions of why I am not good enough. If for no other reason, I simply want to preserve what is left of my self-esteem.

My biggest problem is expecting those that have no capacity for gratitude to express some. I am a sensitive person that cares far too much, and it's going to be a very hard habit to break, to stop caring about these people. Now it's time to let myself grieve the loss of what I thought they were. Despite their constant efforts to indicate that I deserve this much pain, because I only bring it on myself, I will never allow myself to believe that. I have a huge heart, and you did have a place in it. You still could have, had you not been a bunch of cruel and heartless people.

30

THE YEAR AFTER

JULY 8, 2014

It's been a little over a year since the events that landed me in that hell-hole of a hospital. I have made many alterations to my life. Some are really good, positive changes. Some are very hard and painful but had to be made to preserve my sanity.

A lot of people in my life, including family members, made the choice to consistently remind me that they possess no ability whatsoever to show compassion. I truly don't believe they realize that they came very close to losing me forever. Perhaps they just didn't care. I don't know, either way I can't let their ignorance weigh me down any further.

With a lot of hard work, and a lot of support from the

people that do genuinely care, I am better today. I no longer wish I wasn't here anymore. There are days where the struggle just seems to be far too much, and I want to give in. The important thing is that I don't. Even if it's just to show the people out there that believe I can't. I still keep putting one foot in front of the other.

June and July of 2014 have been hard for me. It's been difficult for me to write. I guess I had high hopes that my writing was good enough to become something much bigger, and it hasn't. So I sunk into depression.

Adversity is around every corner, regardless of whether you are bipolar or not. I tend to cower in fear when it strikes. Sooner or later I remember why I do this. I will find strength in the people that have told me that I have helped them, and I feel like just maybe I can keep going. Am I sad? Yes. Am I disappointed? Yes. Will I let this define me? No. You may be like me and choose to hide from the "icky" feelings. Sooner or later you are going to have to come out and face them. Life is full of "icky" feelings, and if you spend your life afraid of processing your depression, grief, sadness, disappointment...well, you'll be hiding forever. What kind of life is that?

I guess I am just a little lost in my own head right now, and that is OK. I just can't set up permanent residence there. I will come out on the other side of this devastation a better person, but it will take time, and I am OK with that.

As far as the difference between this year and last year? I have eliminated so much of the stress, medication, and people that helped me get to that point where I wanted to go to sleep, and if I woke up, whatever, if not...that was fine too. It's been a painful journey, I will not lie to you. If you take away nothing else, just know that not one thing, not one person, not one event is worth losing your life. If someone has a problem with you, it's not your problem. Move on, and enjoy some peace in your life. You deserve it.

31

BITTERNESS AND THE STRUGGLE WITHIN

It's been about a year since I left the hospital, and I use the term "hospital" loosely. I have been struggling with writing this chapter for several weeks. A lot has happened in a year. Much of it has had a positive impact on my life.

I wish I could say it was all sunshine and roses, but it wouldn't be realistic and it wouldn't be true. The other day, I sat down and wrote something that I hoped would be cathartic and get things straight in my head. I hope it will help explain part of what lead me to do what I did, and what I have been going through since. I hope you will keep an open mind, this is a bit different for me.

I laid down on the mattress and filled the very same spot where my mother once laid, stricken with cancer. Lung cancer of all things. After she hadn't smoked in twenty-one years. From June of the year before, until the following January, I cared for my ailing mother. Perhaps I wasn't the best caregiver, but I put every ounce of energy I had into it, when no one else but my father would.

Sitting in the corner in a chair every single day, ready to spring into action and bring my mother anything she might need at any moment. Eventually, I began to realize that I had no medical training, and all of the love in the world wasn't going to help her get better. She needed to go to the hospital to at least get some fluids. Little did any of us know that it would be the last time my mom ever saw her own room.

We called an ambulance to take her to the hospital, but the closest hospital couldn't handle any more patients, so we were directed to one farther away. It was just my mom and I, no one followed, or even seemed that concerned. Denial is a very destructive thing.

I yelled from the front seat, "I am right here, Mom".

She answered back with a meek, "OK", and that was one of the last things she ever said. We got her to the hospital, I encountered a doctor with zero bedside manner. He looked at me, a young woman that was in tears already, "Your mom is a very sick lady" and walked away. They let me see her one last time before they put that thing down her throat. The one thing she was most afraid of. I looked at her, and I was sobbing. She looked up at me and said, "It's OK...it's OK." That was my mom, she was always the strong one.

My mother never spoke again after that. We brought her in on a Thursday and Saturday at 7:00 PM, she was pronounced dead. Each member of our family stood around her bed, holding on to a small piece of her.

I will never forget that day. I relive it like it was yesterday all the time. That was in 2008 and I still cannot come to terms with it. Not only was it the end of my beloved mother's life, but it was the end of life as we knew it. As a family, we always had ups and downs. When I consider what I have been through since her death, all I can say is that she was a saint.

I had no idea that my siblings could be so cruel, callous, and heartless. It wasn't long before the mysterious death of my brother took place, ironically on my birthday. The details are still up in the air, but let's just say he was a lifelong addict. I wasn't doing a magnificent job of keeping the family together as I promised my mom that I would. Now I realize it was just too big of a task for me to take on. These people are not children that need their hand held through everything. They are grown adults who enjoyed a pleasant upbringing and there's no reason for them to treat me, or my mom's memory the way that they do.

Am I still angry? Yes, of course. It's only been a month or so since I severed ties with almost my entire family. It wasn't bad enough that they treated me like an outcast. They went to my father without me present in an attempt to convince my dad that I was off my medications and not thinking clearly. They insinuated I no longer went to the doctor. I see the doctor every three months, and the withdrawal from my medications would nearly kill me. The truth of the matter was, I refused to let them trample on me any longer.

By the way, would it kill you to thank me for taking care of mom for seven months when none of you could find it in your schedule?

It may seem as if I am just writing this to air my dirty laundry. Believe me, if I wanted to do that, people would not remain nameless, and there would be a lot more detail. What these people have put me, my husband, and my father through is unforgivable.

I'm sorry, I try not to be this bitter. I know I've gone over some of this before. I always try to find the silver lining when I write. I'm just in a great deal of pain right now.

At this moment, I am free of harassing text messages and emails, and I have to say, I haven't felt like I could relax up until now. It's sad. I wish I could say there was a way to repair the damage, but I'm afraid it's just not possible.

32

THE PAST

As children, we are always told to keep looking ahead! Your future is so bright, and you have the world at your feet. As adults, we find ourselves mired in the days of yesteryear when things seemed so simple. When the biggest hurdle we had to overcome was whether or not we got to have our best friend spend the night.

I often find myself wondering if we had known more about bipolar disorder, or even just depression as a whole, would I have been able to prepare myself for what lie ahead. Or would we have just swept it under the rug, comfortable in our denial of anything painful.

I see myself now at forty-one years old, and I have trouble looking back at my childhood. Not because it was necessarily painful, but because I mourn for that smaller, happier, care-free version of myself. We've always been told that being an adult isn't easy, and believe me when I tell you that being an adult that is bipolar is even harder. I'm not asking for the easy way out of life, or special treatment, I am just looking for some kindness and consideration.

If babies are born into this world with everyone standing around them oohing and aahing about how "perfect" they are, why on earth do we spend the rest of our days beating them down to have complete and utter lack of self-esteem, confidence, or any idea of what they could have become, had the world not gotten to them first?

As an adult, I still long for the summer time. It reminds me of the days of no school, but you got up at 9:00 am anyway, and you didn't care because all the other kids on the street were up too. You went outside with your agenda for the day, whether it was soccer, slip and slide, or playing Star Wars in your friend's basement. Those days were so long and blissfully happy.

Suddenly, the world became a cruel and unkind place, because you were unlike the status quo. You had a few extra pounds, and were larger than other kids your age, and because of that difference, you no longer fit that happy go lucky, cookie cutter mold. The irony of those days is that, while you spend the rest of your life living in shame because of those differences, you would give anything to go back to the days where you were just a few pounds heavier than the other children. What you've become is so much worse. Perhaps you could have lived with yourself just fine, until people started to take notice that you weren't as thin as the captain of the cheerleaders, or you didn't have the same expensive clothes as the popular kids.

I will always long for those days that started first thing in the morning, and didn't end until the sun went down and the mosquitos came out. I had a happy, memorable childhood, with a few exceptions here and there. I wish I could say the same about my life now.

It's an odd feeling looking back on your life with a sense of joy as tears roll down your cheeks. I don't blame anyone for these negative feelings I have towards myself. I am the biggest part of the problem, quite literally.

I do, however, wish someone would have sat down with me when the warning signs began. Someone could have said, "Look, your life is going to be a mess until you get it through your thick skull that the path you are on will not work for you."

Perhaps I wouldn't have understood it right then, but there would have been that a-ha moment in my life where those words meant everything in the world to me, and I would have just known.

If I could sit down with little me, I would tell her, "You're nuts. Don't ever let anyone tell you anything different. You are absolutely insane, but there are people out there that will love you despite that. You are smart, even though sometimes you won't feel that way. You are beautiful, but I'm telling you right now, all that matters is that you think you are. Do yourself a favor and eat more salads and exercise more. Don't ask, just do it. When you find that adorable, sweet, funny, and amazing man that will sweep you off your feet in his own little way, never let him go."

I bet I would have listened.

33

PAIN

For many years, the phrase, "I have a headache" was just a comical excuse to get out of sex with your significant other. It was most often used by women, so I don't think most men comprehend the impact that headaches can have on your quality of life. In my experience, a lot of women can't grasp the concept either. They are fortunate enough to not ever have had to deal with a real migraine headache and the aftermath.

Mine started when I was about twelve. I had a math teacher who would let me go sit in a dark room adjacent to his classroom if it got unbearable. His wife had them too, so he understood. Coincidentally, I also had just recently gotten braces, so I always wondered if there was a correlation.

My teens were not excruciating as far as headaches went, but once I hit my twenties, they doubled in duration, intensity, and frequency. By the time I turned twenty-eight, and I was about to get married, I was getting probably five to ten a month. It seemed like each year they got worse in one way or another. We moved in 2002, and after that I would get these marathon migraines that would last for four to five days, and I always ended up in the ER.

I had been complaining about these issues since I was twelve, but no doctor was ever able to offer the correct advice. I've been on many medications, stopped taking aspirin, only to have the headaches quadruple, and been to the ER so many times I can't even count anymore. Not to mention, tried several different types of eyeglasses. For a while there, I was taking a medication that worked about 85% of the time, which was a relief for me. Eventually, it started producing crippling side effects that I just couldn't deal with anymore, so here I am, back at square one.

The last time I was placed in psychiatric care, I spoke with a nurse practitioner there that had spent a great deal of time working with a neurologist. I told her that no one could figure out why this kept happening. She looked at me as sternly as anyone ever has and said,

"Honey, there is no reason for you to keep getting these migraines. You have migraine brain. You were born with it, and it's never going to go away".

I guess in the back of my mind, I always knew that was the case. I mean when you're in the ER on Morphine and your head still hurts, you're probably up the proverbial creek without a paddle.

This is why I get aggravated when people give me all of their fantastic herbal remedies, or the number of the best doctor ever, or suggest some new medication. It's a give and take, I guess. As sick as they are of hearing about my headaches, is how sick I am of hearing about their miracle cures.

This is just something I am going to have to manage, just like my depression. It's going to mess things up, cause me a lot of pain, and probably piss a lot of people off, but I don't have time to worry about that anymore. I have to worry about having some type of life despite all of the obstacles placed in front of me.

So, there you have it. When I say I have a headache, I'm not screwing around trying to be funny. I am probably in horrible, excruciating, blinding pain with no end in sight. It's OK for you to say, I hope you feel better. Just please don't tell me what your best friend's cousin twice removed that is related to a doctor told her to do and it worked this one time. I don't care. Not to be an ass, but it's the truth. I just don't. What I care about is working through it, like I always do, and coming out on the other end pain free. Yes, at this point I am at about ten to twelve headaches per month, but guess what? That's down from fifteen, so I guess I'll take that as a good sign.

It's like I've said before, you can't possibly walk a mile in my shoes, or anyone else's. They don't fit, and you would be bitching to get them off in about a minute and a half, so don't even try. Just be there to understand, and maybe once in a while check in and see how that person is doing. None of us is asking you to fix it. We just want to be understood.

34

DEADLINES

JULY 19, 2014

All too often, we put deadlines and restrictions on our lives, not even realizing that we are setting ourselves up to fail. We will make a to-do list five pages long and wonder why we feel no sense of accomplishment at even taking on two or three of the tasks. Take a step back and think for just a minute about what you are doing.

Have you spent so much of your life expecting yourself to fail, that you barely know what it is to succeed anymore? What if that list had one single item on it? You would feel guilty, wouldn't you? Worthless somehow. I know those feelings all too well.

Let me tell you a little story about a moment in time in my life. Everything had seemed to spiral out of control for me. My family life, my finances, my health, and especially my depression symptoms. I am a very neat person. I generally clean my house every single day, and nobody is allowed in here if it isn't. OCD? Probably, but we'll save that for another day.

About six days passed and I hadn't cleaned the house not once. I didn't vacuum a room, I didn't dust, and I barely even stacked the dishes in the sink. You know what happened? Nothing. Absolutely nothing. My world didn't come crashing down around me, my husband didn't leave me, and we didn't develop a bug infestation. Nobody showed up on my doorstep from the show, "Hoarders". Life as we know it went on just as if I had been tending to those things all along.

It was an epiphany for me. Would I want it to go any longer than that? Good Lord, no. However, all of these impossible deadlines I put on myself were causing me nothing but heartache and pain. They were supposed to leave me with a sense of accomplishment. I have come to the realization that I can say to myself, OK...today is Tuesday. Today, you will try to recuperate. You will try to find your center and dig deep down for the energy you so lack right now, and the first thing you will do, is wash the dishes. That's it. No more, no less.

Should Wednesday roll around and I still do not feel as if I can get out of that bed and find the momentum I need, then I need a smaller goal. We'll reduce it to just getting out of bed. There will be no guilt, there will be no one standing over you telling you that you are not good enough...that you are not enough, period.

I can't promise you that what I write will help everyone. I am not a professional, I have no formal schooling, but what I can tell you is how each experience has worked on me. I am my own personal guinea pig. Do yourself a favor, until you feel stronger and more confident, throw the lists right out the window. As I said in the beginning, you are setting yourself up for failure and an even longer bout with depression. Just give it a try.

35

THE OK DAY

There are times when you are bipolar that you can physically stop yourself, flip through the pages of your mind, and come to a conclusion. I am OK. Right now, at this moment, I have all I need, and I feel good. You put away all of the what if thinking that has you worried what tomorrow will bring. You live in that moment, and damn it's a good feeling.

My OK Day was yesterday. I stopped for a moment and remembered how completely in love I am in with my husband, and that through everything, I will forever be grateful for his presence in my life. He had just left the house to run an errand, and I needed him to know that I was OK. I sent him a text thanking him for being my knight in shining armor. That is what he is to me.

So, now that you have found your moment of bliss, the next thing you or your loved ones say is, "Let's hope it lasts a little while." It's a typical reaction. It would be phenomenal if the path to a happy life was paved with hope. Once that statement is made, the tiny little bit of logic I have resting somewhere in my brain reminds me to stop. Don't hope for more. Live with what you have right now.

I learned a long time ago that one of the biggest traits that my depression brings out in me is the fear of failure. One thing goes wrong, and that's it. I failed again.

So, I say to myself when I am fortunate enough to realize I am on that path, *don't hope. Don't even consider what the future will bring, just be here in this moment.*

Ironically enough, most people reach out and hold onto hope like it's their life line. I cannot. What happens if I don't have another good day tomorrow? What if I spent my one good opportunity just hoping for the next?

It creeps up on me slowly, but it's always there. The F word. You failed. Another hope, dream, goal, and plan for your future is unattainable because you let your depression steal it from you. And whether this makes sense to the average person or not, our brains will turn this into our biggest screw up yet.

Regret and guilt will soon follow, and you wonder if you were ever really happy at all. I know how crazy it all sounds. When I say crazy, I mean silly, odd, strange, and even peculiar. Not mentally ill. Even as I write this, I wonder who will truly understand.

Everything I write has a purpose, and because of that, I feel like everything I write has an audience. Even if these words reach one person who has felt as I have, I've succeeded in what I was trying to do.

And for that reason, and many others, I finally had my OK Day.

36

MOOD SWINGS

JULY 30, 2014

Sometimes I feel like I am on the playground swinging back and forth on the swing set. Up and I feel alright, down and I am thoroughly depressed. It's almost as if my body has a physical reaction to my mood swings now. I've become so accustomed to them over the years. One minute, all could appear to be right with the world, and the next minute all I can think about is what is wrong with it.

We have these strange days occasionally here in the summer, where it will be raining and the sun will be shining at the same time. In speaking about this earlier today, it occurred to me that days like this are very much like a metaphor for depression. The sun may be shining, but in my world it's still raining.

I've been dealing with writer's block for a while now, and it was only until today... just in the last hour, when I felt my mood shifting, that I knew what to write about. It starts with an overwhelming exhaustion, loss of concentration and a need to escape. Why take everyone around me down with me?

Lately, I have been feeling a painful sense of being abandoned whenever I am feeling down. I am grateful to those that have stuck by me through the worst of times, but still angry at those that could only handle the best of times. Why was I the one that was called selfish? Why not those that took off because they couldn't handle the sadness, the pain, the depression? That feels much more selfish to me than someone who can't possibly control a chemical imbalance in their brain.

I know I am far too ready to call a spade a spade, even when perhaps a spade was a queen of hearts. I am prone to overreacting, but I have noticed that trait also comes and goes like mood swings.

Even now, it's difficult for me to focus, hard to find the words. I keep reaching for my sarcasm to get me through because if I didn't I would probably dissolve into tears and curl up in the fetal position. Moments like this terrify me, and here you are enjoying the fruits of my terror. Rain is falling outside, and that couldn't be more appropriate.

As you can see, my thoughts are scattered. It's a battle just to keep my fingers moving across the keyboard. I want to give this minor crisis in my life a voice. Perhaps I will learn something about myself. Perhaps you will learn something about yourself. When I am down, I am so far down it seems as if there is no return. All I have the strength to do is sleep. Of course, when I need it most, it so rarely comes because my brain is stuck on repeat. It's moments like this that have me questioning, why? Why me? Why now?

I genuinely wish there was an answer. Why do some of us carry this burden, while others have glorious, happy lives and do marvelous things without even a moment of sadness? Yes, that may be an exaggeration of sorts, but you get the idea. I get it, OK? I understand that only the strong survive, but if I could trade happiness for strength, would that be fair? Would I be happy with that decision? I would love to test the theory, just for a day.

As I glance out the window and see that now the sun shines amidst the raindrops, I know I will come out of this. It will be OK. The trick is not to expect too much too soon. This weight in my chest will get lighter, and these crazy, racing thoughts will dissipate. I've got over twenty years of experience on my side. I can do it. You can too.

37

THE STORM

There comes a time when despite your best efforts to avoid further chaos in your life, you are faced with a crisis. Regardless of your emotional state, you have to find a way to maintain your sanity and weather the storm. In my case, it just so happens that this crisis involved my father. He will be turning eighty-five on September twentieth. As far as someone who is eighty-four is concerned, he is in good health. However, he does suffer from terrible memory loss and has occasionally been known to pass out. A few weeks ago, he proceeded down to the basement in his house, lost his balance, and fell. The floor in the basement is made of concrete. By the time I heard about it, he was in the ER at the hospital nearby and was just a mess.

Ever since my mom passed away, and I was institutionalized, I find it extremely difficult to set foot in any hospital. Let alone the one that had me committed. Walking into that place brought back every unpleasant feeling that I had been trying to avoid. On top of those feelings of sheer terror, and the burning in my stomach, you can add the fear that I was also going to lose my dad. I'm just not ready for that. I know nobody is ever ready to lose a loved one, but since I still haven't recovered from losing my mom and my brother, I am even less likely to recover from the loss of my father.

Thankfully, when I entered the ER where he was being treated, I found him awake and reasonably aware. He was somewhat confused and kept talking about strange things. However, judging by the enormous cut on his head, and his torn up little body, this was no shock to me. I so wanted to stay with him, and talk him through this. Yet, I so needed to get out of there. It's a horrible, horrible feeling. Knowing that you can't be there for someone 100% because you are so lost in the maze of your own fears.

Since that day, my dad has been moved a couple of times and has had surgery on his neck. They removed four sections of his neck and replaced them with metal rods. Had he not had the surgery, and he fell again, he would have been paralyzed. His current status is that he has physical therapy every day. He is in a neck brace, his right hand is broken, and his left hand still hasn't returned to a functional state.

Every time we go see him, he recalls a letter that I wrote him this year for Father's Day. I decided that I wasn't going to get him a card, I was going to write him a heartfelt letter. Apparently, he had forgotten about it and discovered it on his desk a few days before his accident. He cries every time he recalls my words. He said to me, "Boy, you're a real writer. I didn't know you felt that way. I feel the same way about you". Despite myself, I had to smile. I knew that now he was truly aware of my feelings for him.

The best part? I knew that he was proud of me, and now looked at me in a new way because he knows I possess the ability to write. What an amazing gift to receive through such a tragedy.

I still have tremendous difficulty going to see him. It's very hard to see the one person that has always been your Superman, in that state. Not to mention, I have to deal with the possibility of seeing family members that I have severed ties with. If I can't get there to see him, we call him and one of the nurses holds the phone up to his ear. We are hoping he is released before his birthday. I am working through my fear, and with the support of my husband, I hope to come to terms with the situation. I love my father, and I am grateful that he now knows without a shadow of a doubt how much.

True strength is not necessarily found where you would hope. It is found in the subtle nuances of your daily life. Every day that you wake up, and summon the energy to live, you are finding strength. Now that you have lived through another catastrophe, you can breathe a sigh of relief.

38

I AM ENOUGH

OCTOBER 19, 2014

I don't really remember a time when I wasn't experiencing some type of turmoil in my life. I grew up with 4 older brothers and an older sister. They all took their fair share of recreational drugs or drank alcohol. They caused my parents many sleepless nights. Unfortunately, at an early age I began to experience the anxiety that would also cause me to lose sleep. I don't think I had a fair shot at a healthy existence. Not for lack of trying.

As the years went on, I knew something was a little off with me too. Being overweight and made fun of a lot in middle school didn't help. High school went a little better. I suppose I could have been considered popular. I certainly wasn't an outcast. Yet, by the age of 19, my suspicion that I wasn't wired quite right became a fact. I was depressed, and there wasn't a thing I could do to fix it.

I started seeing my first psychiatrist then. I remember the first medication I was ever prescribed was Prozac. I honestly don't recall if it helped or for how long. It was just the beginning of an arduous journey through the county health system. At the time, I didn't have mental health coverage, so I had to take what I could get. It worked out alright for several years. They really didn't give a damn about you, but you didn't have to pay for your medications. I always lived by the motto, "Beggars can't be choosers".

With the depression came horrible anxiety. Borderline Personality Disorder would soon follow, along with PTSD. The older I got, the worse I got. There came a time when I was on 7 medications at once. I found myself drifting in a sea of worthless relationships with men that made me feel like a freak. In 1998, I was in a long distance relationship that began online. He asked me to marry him. Before that could happen, but after the deposits had been put down, he dumped me. Apparently a psychotic episode and a psychiatric hospitalization make you less appealing to the opposite sex.

With his hasty exit from my life weighing heavily on my shoulders, I taught myself self-injury. I didn't know that's what it was at the time. I didn't know anyone else knew what it was either. Ironically, I discovered it when I was rejected by another male acquaintance, and I had it in my head that life wasn't worth living. It was an accident really. A failure of sorts that became a coping mechanism when things were too much for me to handle.

I realize as I look back on the past that it most certainly appears that I just didn't experience a single happy moment in my entire life. That isn't true. I found happiness quite frequently. I held some gratifying positions with successful companies. I was often promoted and thought of to be a problem solver. I partied on the weekends, I met famous people, I went to concerts and sporting events. I had a best friend that I met in 5th grade that was a constant in my life. We were never apart for long, no matter what path we chose for ourselves.

I made new friends and met a lot of people online. You know, in the 90's when it wasn't quite as terrifying as it is now. Back then, not once did I think I was talking to a pedophile or a stalker. I was lucky that everyone I met was who they said they were.

The problem with my life was that as happy as it could be, the misery was a thousand times worse. I didn't ever put two and two together. It never occurred to me that I couldn't just take a bunch of medication and go on about my business and I would be all better. I didn't understand that I had to do the work too.

Once I made that realization, I started to make better choices. I stopped meeting multiple people online. I buckled down and worked really hard. I met someone that although at first we didn't seem compatible, we eventually discovered that we missed each other once we were apart. In 2001, we were married. Thirteen years later, he still knows how to make me laugh. We are happy, even though I still have my highs and my lows. I would be lost without him. My calming force in a sea of chaos.

Although I have spent over 20 years dealing with a multitude of mental health disorders, I am ALIVE. I consider myself a survivor. A warrior to say the least. Every day I wake up and hope that it will be a good day. Unfortunately, not every day can be. Thankfully, I am learning to process the guilt a bad day brings. I am learning that I didn't ask for this, and I certainly wouldn't wish it on my worst enemy. But, I can do this. If only people could understand how much energy goes into fighting this fight.

In the last 20 years, I've experienced more pain than anyone should ever have to bear. The death of my mother brought me to my knees. The more recent death of my brother, sent me on a tailspin. Yet, despite the outside influences that could have and should have broken me, I still fight on. I see the doctor, I take my medication. I give my feelings a voice no matter how hard it is, and I keep waking up every day with just a tiny glimmer of hope.

There may be days when I look in the mirror and feel like a failure. Sometimes, I want to give up. Then, I remember the strength it took to get me to this point in my life.

I remember I AM ENOUGH.

39

WRITER'S BLOCK

OCTOBER 22, 2014

Now and then, I wake up in the morning feeling the need to put words to paper. I imagine what the topic will be, or the way the first sentence will read. It feels good. Like a power that I can harness on my laptop using Microsoft Word. Then, I sit down at my desk, turn on the computer and stare at a blank screen for half an hour.

Sometimes I feel almost as if one of the great literary works of our time is going to come flowing from my mind and into my working fingers. I imagine happiness that above all else and despite any obstacles I have attained due to my incredible knack for the written word.

Then my brain replies back, "Yeah...not so much". It isn't as if I can't think of a single thing to write about. I have too much to write about and no clear cut way of making any sense in the process. I often refer to it as writer's block. Is that it, or is it just one more way that my depression keeps me from happiness.

If you look up "racing thoughts" online, you will often be directed to Generalized Anxiety Disorder (GAD). I know and understand that this is part of my diagnosis. It is excessive, out-of-control worrying about every-day things. Are my racing thoughts about all of my possible writing topics really just me worrying about anything and everything?

It doesn't feel that way in the moment, but perhaps it's something that I need to consider. The most difficult part of this condition is the desire to just give up if I can't calm the images in my mind. It's too hard, so I give up writing that day. Maybe that is the best solution to help preserve my sanity. Those of us experiencing depression on a daily basis already have so much to struggle with. I don't think I need to add something that will send the pile spilling over into oblivion.

I have been asked to guest blog for a few different websites. I want to do it with every fiber of my being. However, the fear is always inside of me...what if I can't keep up? I went years without writing a single word on a piece of paper. Suppose I fall back into the same pattern, and I can't fulfill my obligations? It terrifies me. I am all too aware that this fear will eventually lead to feelings of failure.

I don't ever want this disease to become the excuse that keeps me from real life. On good days, I want to conquer the world. On bad days, I need to take one step at a time, feeling lucky if I remember to eat. I long to find a balance. So, I will take each day as it comes. Hope for more good than bad, and figure it out as I go. I plan on looking back at each chapter, paragraph and sentence as me overcoming my fear of the unknown.

I think I can be happy with that for now.

40

DROWNING

NOVEMBER 6, 2014

I'm lost. I can't see anything in front of me, except darkness. The weight on my chest is unbearable, and I can no longer breathe. I'm drowning, mired in this metaphorical ocean of instability. Most of the time, I can reach out for a tiny sense of hope. At that moment, I know that if I could just get this, this and this to follow through, everything will be OK.

Today, there is no "this" and there certainly isn't any hope. It's such a simple thing. A small mistake that has spread like a disease. I've been awake most of the night trying to find a solution, and I am afraid I have not been successful. For once in my life, I can't think my way out of it.

I'm so very tired and sad. Why does it seem as if no

matter how hard I try, I can't get ahead of it all? Am I having a pity party? I don't know. Whose business is it? If you aren't paying my bills or taking care of my family, I don't care about your opinions. I just wish I could find the strength to swim to shore, and find my way out of this mess.

I spend so much time trying to help others so that they don't have to follow my path and go through these feelings of defeat, fear...failure. I would love to be able to talk myself down from the ledge. It's 2:58 am, and here I'm stuck in every way. I don't think I can find a positive conclusion to reach this time. At this point in my life, nothing seems the least bit positive.

I have no answers to any of these questions, and for a person with control issues, that is a terrifying experience. All I can ask is that I at least make it out of this in one piece. I'm going to try, but whatever strength I had has long since left me.

41

THERE'S A NAME
FOR THAT

Do you remember when you were a kid, and you would find yourself excited about the smallest things? The sound of the ice cream man coming up the street sent you into fits. Forget about how over the moon you were the night before Christmas or the day of your birthday party. I remember just lying in my bed and dreaming of how amazing it was going to be when I got everything I asked for.

Fast forward 30 years, and you don't have a whole lot to be excited about anymore. Occasionally, the idea of spending a girl's night out or having a date night with your significant other gets your spirits up. Mostly, you start to realize that you aren't getting "excited" about average things. Instead, the feelings that you used to describe as butterflies in your stomach now come at the most inappropriate times and don't make you feel any happiness.

If you've been dealing with it for years, you can probably recognize that it feels an awful lot like an anxiety attack. Giving it a name doesn't give you a reason for it. Suppose it's Saturday, and you know Monday that you have to go see the dentist. You hate the dentist. He might be the nicest dentist you've ever met, but you've had more bad experiences than good with your teeth. Suddenly, you are overcome with what can only be characterized as terror. Your appointment isn't even for a couple more days. What is going on?

Well, I recently discovered something. There's a name for that, and it's called Anticipatory Anxiety. I'm willing to bet that the crippling effects of this condition have kept you away from more appointments, gatherings, and events than you can count. So what exactly is it? I've done some research, and I feel the following definition puts it all together quite well.

Anticipatory Anxiety is apprehension about an event prior to its occurrence. For example, death, danger, or poor evaluation by others. Often, this is accompanied by physiological symptoms such as rapid heart rate or muscle tension. It may also occur in Panic Disorder where an individual fears another panic attack[1].

Are you sitting there telling yourself that this all sounds very familiar? That was the same reaction I had. It's difficult to determine whether this is good news or bad. Now that there's a name for it, shouldn't we be able to avoid it? Some people would lead us to believe that. However, I've been through episodes where I wasn't even thinking about anything that could lead me to these feelings, but I got them regardless.

There have been times when I feel like I'm constantly being judged by the outside world. Especially when it comes to a particular diagnosis. I don't want it to appear that I am just collecting conditions to use as an excuse later. I would prefer that people consider what this situation is. I am trying to learn the most I can about my condition so that I can improve my quality of life. Being honest about what is plaguing me is certainly not trying to find an excuse out of my responsibilities or my life.

---

[1] "What is ANTICIPATORY ANXIETY? Definition of ANTICIPATORY ANXIETY (psychology dictionary)."

I resent anyone who would think otherwise. If I could snap my fingers and feel "normal", I would do it in a heartbeat. I would hope that any of my real friends would know that. I certainly don't sit around deciding that I don't want to go somewhere or do something, so that day I will pretend to be suffering a panic attack.

What people need to know is that there is a physical as well as an emotional aspect to this horrible disease. While some of us may be better suited to control the symptoms at different times, there will be instances where we have no control over anything. That is what scares me the most. Losing control over whatever tiny little bit of my life that I thought I could handle.

Every single day is a battle. Not every battle can be fought and won. I long for people to understand that.

42

WINTER BLUES

NOVEMBER 16, 2014

I think it's time I start facing the fact that winter is here again. I've never enjoyed cold weather. As long as I can remember, I've been terrified of driving in the snow. All I feel up to doing is hiding in my house. I know that I've been in a state of denial since about the middle of September. Just allowing myself to consider what is in store is causing a physical reaction. I'm nauseated and very nervous. On the cusp of a nasty panic attack.

Approaching Thanksgiving once again, I am struck by how much I miss what used to be. I never thought I would be in this position. Very little family to connect with and certainly no close friends to invite over. The only person I have even considered seeing is my dad. I would like to invite him over, but he is in a lot of pain these days, and it might not be possible. When he took that fall in August, I had a feeling life would change forever for all of us.

I grew up with a large family. Four older brothers and one older sister. Gradually, the family got larger as they married or had children. Now, with every one of their marriages disintegrated, and a lifetime of bitterness between all of us, we will probably never spend another holiday together. I looked forward to adding my little family to the group once Joe and I married. We are the only ones left standing. Who would have thought?

I can't even imagine putting up the Christmas tree this year. I don't know if I can do this. Any of it. I'm afraid. So very scared. I'm attempting to force my way through for the sake of my husband. I took his family away by just my very existence. I have lived for the moment when he opens his gifts for years. This year, with finances not looking so good, I can't even begin to start my online quest for a good deal. I'm not going to lie; I am hiding all of this from everyone.

I can't face any more disappointed faces. I can't explain why "I just can't" anymore. I'm bored with myself and my irrational illness. So very fed up with the various stages of uncontrollable sadness. I know there are people out there that honestly believe that a person can just say, "I'm going to be happy" and it happens. Maybe those people do exist, but in my world such a person is as fictitious as a unicorn or a leprechaun. You would like to think the whimsy and wonder of such a being exists, but you'll never see it.

I've done that. I've pushed the dark thoughts to the back of my mind far too many times to count. I've told myself that you are going to be happy and enjoy your life starting...NOW. You know what happened? Not a damn thing, because I am not one of those people.

So, this year I guess I will just "get through" once again. I'll find a way because that is the only choice I have. I can't give up because who knows how much time on this Earth my father has left? I won't give up because the one man that means everything to me needs me to stick with it. For those two reasons, I will make it through the winter, the holidays and the birthdays of those no longer with us. No matter how difficult it is. Maybe I'll find some joy this year.

43

THE ANGER INSIDE ME

DECEMBER 18, 2014

I am angry. Let me say that again, **I AM ANGRY!** It repeats over and over again in my brain until it consumes me. The type of anger that is so fierce, it's almost as if you can see it. You can certainly feel it. Carrying it around as I do every single day, it now seems like a part of me, like another limb. I could sit around for days and list why I am angry.

I don't intend on doing that. At least, at this point and time I don't.

I have a struggle going on inside of my brain nearly 24 hours a day. The part of me that is desperately trying to find sense in all of these emotions keeps attempting to tell the other part of me to stop thinking about it. You have this or that to be grateful for. The anger has just grown too strong. For every positive, there are ten negatives and common sense is beaten down until it can't fight anymore.

I've tried to reach out, to give my feelings words, to explain myself. It's not helping. It's not even scratching the surface. The worst part is, for a brief moment I can tell myself, this isn't the time of year for this. Try to find some joy in the season. You know what that does for me? Makes me positively irate. For the reasons I feel this way and the people who have brought me down to their level.

I'm not a stupid person. I understand that if you wake up every single day feeling overwhelmed with anger, you are not going to be able to make your life or anyone else's life the least bit pleasant. That is the dilemma I face. I've been mad before, furious even. This is different. There is a physical pain on the inside of me that just makes me want to scream as loud as I can.

I don't have a therapist. This book is my therapist. Even if I did see a therapist, I doubt I would receive much relief at this point. I am too stuck in the "Yeah...but..." stage of it all. If you come at me with a response, no matter how logical, I am going to yeah but you to death until you give up from sheer exhaustion.

The feelings I have now make me understand revenge. That need that builds up inside of you. You can't stop thinking about the desired target, or what you'll do once you finally stand face to face with it. My problem is, I am pretty well convinced that my target is my life. I could backtrack and pinpoint certain people in my life. Exacting revenge against them would surely be sweet, but that is just not the kind of person I am. All I am saying is that I get it. I understand the desire.

With no answers in sight and the number of questions growing by the day, I know I have to find a way out of this. My usual "coping skills", which are not coping skills at all, are no longer an option for me. As I pat myself on the back for finding the courage to not turn to the darkest place I know, I find myself once again back where I started. If it wasn't for this, that or the other thing, I wouldn't even have these thoughts.

Of all the cycles I have seen in my life, this is by far the most vicious. I know that I have got to find a way to stop it. Each time I write, I try to find a silver lining of sorts. If not that, I attempt to come to a conclusion that could help me. This is all that I have to offer: I am aware that this anger is eating away at me, at my life, at my happiness.

I will strive to do whatever I can to simply let it go. However painful the process will be, I know that I can make it through it.

44

AM I MANIC?

JANUARY 18, 2015

I'm in a good place right now. It isn't often that I get to say that, and certainly never out loud. When most people get up in the morning feeling good, they understand that they're in a good mood, and never give it a second thought. Most people never have to stop to wonder, they just know. There's a part of me that will always question whether or not I am heading into a manic episode, otherwise known as mania.

I'm laughing a lot, sometimes at nonsensical things. I'm staying up too late, walking around singing, and reminiscing about the good old days. Quite possibly, I am in denial about a few things too. I'm getting a lot done during the day, and I seem to have a lot of energy out of nowhere.

Mania typically occurs as a symptom of bipolar disorder. Individuals experiencing a manic episode often have feelings of self-importance, elation, talkativeness, sociability, and a desire to embark on goal-oriented activities, coupled with the less desirable characteristics of irritability, impatience, impulsiveness, hyperactivity, and a decreased need for sleep[2].

I know for certain a few of those apply to me at this point. So, the question remains...should I continue to question where I'm at because inevitably there will be a crash, or do I just go with it, and enjoy the ride?

How I wish I didn't have to spend every day of my life interpreting my own moods, and trying to plan for the possibilities. This is my life and like it or not, these are the cards I've been dealt. It's the crash I fear most of all. There's no considering if it will happen, only when and how badly. As my thoughts begin to race, I have more and more trouble focusing on the task at hand.

Someday perhaps very soon, I will find myself deep in the depths of despair. I don't mean to sound as if I am dwelling on that eventuality, but I must force myself

---

[2] "Mania." *TheFreeDictionary.com*. Web. <http://medicaldictionary.thefreedictionary.com/mania>.

to be realistic and prepare for the worst. I worry the most for my husband, who has been able to reap the benefits of my heightened mood, but will also suffer the consequences of my depression. What a tangled web this disease weaves. Being happy but not being able to enjoy the happiness? Well, that's borderline ridiculous. Sometimes being so self-aware is a curse in itself.

Today I can safely say that while I know in my heart that I have entered a state of mania, I truly and wholeheartedly fear for my future. I will push those feelings to the back of my mind once again and just hope. Sometimes that is all I have to hold onto is hope.

I will continue to be optimistic about what 2015 holds for me, but at the same time I am guarded. This could be one of the worst years of my life, or it could be a great year. It simply depends on the sequence of events. I won't attempt to predict the future. For now, I will continue to live my life the best I know how, and try my best not to be so hard on myself.

45

LOVE IN A BIPOLAR WORLD

FEBRUARY 4, 2015

When you find that special person that you know you want to spend the rest of your life with, you have to consider a lot of factors. If you are bipolar, the list of considerations changes quite a bit. Should you tell that person up front? Will it scare them away? What if you don't tell them, and you experience depression, anxiety, even mania?

I know in my situation, I met a couple of guys before I met my husband, and I was always brutally honest. I never kept my condition from anyone. I was sure to make it clear that there was nothing easy about my situation, and there would be ups and downs. If the discussion ever warranted, I also made sure that they knew that kids were not in my future.

Some seemed to think they could handle it, but truthfully couldn't. The first time my depression kicked in, they stopped calling. Others were long gone before I finished the words, bipolar disorder. Joe was different from the start. He was kind and caring. He seemed to accept my issues. He came from a strong Catholic background, and I knew it would be hard to sell me to his parents, specially with no grandchildren in the mix.

It didn't take very long for Joe to realize that perhaps I wasn't right for him. He suddenly dropped out of the picture, and I was left confused and alone. I hoped my disease wasn't what scared him off, but deep down, I knew it was. Not many people know that about us. Our first time trying to make a go of it, we just didn't click. I suffered through a series of mentally and sometimes physically abusive relationships after that. I convinced myself that this was the best I could do.

In May 2001, Joe started calling again. I was guarded because I didn't want the past to repeat itself. My parents were thrilled, especially my mom. She had always liked Joe and she was constantly worried about the other guys I chose to spend my time with.

Joe confessed to me that he hadn't been able to stop thinking about me. That a couple of years earlier, he wasn't grown up enough to understand what challenges I would bring to the table. We worked harder at a relationship this time around, and by the end of July we were talking about marriage and moving in together.

When I look back on my failed relationships, I absolutely cringe. I should never have settled for the pain and heartache I had to endure. My self-esteem was so far in the toilet. I just knew that since I wasn't truly good enough for anyone, that men could treat me as such. I just accepted it. After you subject yourself to this for years, if something good comes along, you can hardly recognize it, let alone believe it's actually happening.

I'm here to tell you that you do not have to allow yourself to be treated like you aren't worth it. You are not broken, useless or a failure. You have just as much to offer this world as anyone who doesn't suffer from mental illness. There will probably always be that little voice inside your head telling you that this one is going to walk out on you too. Don't let that voice take over!

Relationships are hard for anyone. They are even more difficult on those of us with bipolar. I'm not going to tell you that it's always perfect. Once you find the love of your life, it's pretty damn close. Honesty, communication, and laughter. You must have all of these. Talk about your feelings! Give them a voice. Know that your spouse loves you for you, and for the happiness you bring into their life. When you get down, don't do what I've done in the past and offer them a way out. It hurts them more than it hurts you.

Anything worth fighting for is hard work, we all know this. When you find love and acceptance in the eyes of your best friend, you will know true happiness. Don't doubt yourself or your relationship. You will, of course, have ups and downs, there is no way around that. Everyone does! Yours will be a different set of challenges, and you must be realistic about that. Just know that you can do this.

All of my life, I have struggled to find something that I am actually good at. I have finally found it. Loving my husband so completely is my calling in life. He means everything to me, and I can only hope that each and every person reading this can find that as well. Being married with mental illness is not impossible. It takes work, but it is more than worth it.

46

FROM A DISTANCE

FEBRUARY 12, 2015

Most people are aware of the fact that I hate birthdays. I hate getting older, and I hate losing people that I love because they have gotten older. It is also not lost on me that some of the most horrible things that have ever happened to me occurred on my birthday. So, when I start to consider the possibilities of having a birthday party, I'm torn. Perhaps I should just let this one go this year. 42 really isn't a special number. Then a part of me remembers that I could not have made it to this age, and I would like to celebrate that fact.

In my head, I start to make up a guest list. However, when I put it to paper, I am overcome by a harsh realization. Anyone that I would possibly invite to a party, well honestly they are Joe's friends. Of course, over time they have become my friends, and for that I am grateful. I can recall a time when I had a relatively long list of my own friends that I brought into the marriage that I could invite. Those people have long since left my life.

I have one friend, but she lives out of state and probably wouldn't be able to make it. It's easier for me to tell myself that because if she said no, I would certainly feel rejected by my only friend. This is what keeps me awake at night. Have I spent so much of my life pushing people away that there is quite simply, no one left? Am I really that horrible of a person? Don't I possess any redeeming qualities at all?

I know I am quick to anger and accuse. So many people have hurt me in the past; I can't help but expect the worst. Perhaps I spend so much time assuming that they can't help but buckle under my expectations.

Do I push everyone away? Is it easier for me to face life not ever having to compromise when I surely don't want to? I have no family nearby that I speak to, except my father. He's 85 now and quite possibly may have dementia. Everyone else is out of state or cut out of my life. It's times like this that I question everything. Why am I not good enough?

I've given people that have hurt me chance after chance. The outcome was always the same. They hurt me again. I've spoken of it often, but my suicide attempt in 2013 most assuredly scared off several friends, even those that had been around for 20 or more years. I came out of the hospital to discover that I had lost several close friends due to my mental illness. At this point, I'm really not sure which way is up.

I would never want anyone that I do consider a friend to think that I didn't care about them or respect our relationship. Of course, I do. I simply don't have anyone in my life that I frequently see or spend time with. Some of the people I consider close friends, I've never even met. What does that say about me? Am I just better from a distance?

When I begin to second guess all of my choices, and start to miss those that have departed, I have to slap myself back to reality. I am aware that there was a reason for all of this; it's just hard to see when you are so very lonely and sad. I frequently tell myself that I let people go to preserve what is left of my sanity. It's true. I've committed myself to the belief that I would rather spend my days with my husband and my cats.

Perhaps I just need to accept that this is my life. I have allowed this to happen. I need to take full responsibility for my actions. I guess the hardest part about this whole situation is knowing that I let people walk into my life, stomp all over me and then strut all the way back out again. It's stupid really. I guess I just look back to the house full of people we had here for Christmas a few years ago and wonder where I went wrong.

To our friends that have stuck by me, thank you. I don't know where I would be without you. Your support and love has not gone unnoticed. I promise to use my past mistakes as lessons and try very hard not to push you away.

47

A DEVASTATING DEFEAT

MARCH 3, 2015

I have spent the better part of the last four months driving my husband crazy, making sure he checked the mail every single day, without fail. I was expecting something that I thought was going to change my life. I hoped it would change a lot of lives. Perhaps, it would make ours better. I would have finally achieved a goal that I had been trying to obtain since I was in third grade. On November 1, 2014 a publishing company told me that they had every intention of publishing my book.

They welcomed me to the family and told me that my contract would be on the way. At first, I checked in with my contact frequently. Eventually, I would email him at the first of every month because I still hadn't received my contract. I was promised every time, that despite some difficulties they were having, they had not forgotten about me. I was still going to be published.

I held onto that. Probably for much longer than I should have. Finally, after reaching out once again on March 2, 2015 five months after first being notified of the deal, I received an email from someone I've never spoken to before. She indicated that despite what I had been told, there was no contract, and there never would be.

Even if they wanted to publish my book, they couldn't because they don't publish "those" types of books anymore. Good luck.

It was gone. My dream was smashed into a million pieces, and there wasn't a damn thing I could do about it. I had absolutely no hope. I cried off and on for three days. I still cry at the drop of a hat. The few people that responded when I posted the news online, really didn't comprehend the magnitude of the situation.

They don't understand that telling me not to give up, or to publish it myself isn't helping. It isn't as if I sought out one publishing company and when it fell through, I gave up. Initially, I did try to publish it myself. This costs money that we don't have. I was able to secure a few donations, but I never made a profit on the book, and honestly it was a joke. It wasn't professional, and my work needed more editing.

After that, I had someone who was a publisher that I was working with. This proved to be a frustrating and insulting experience. I finally told her that we had to part ways.

For nearly a year after that, I contacted other publishing companies and was either turned down or discovered that they would charge me thousands of dollars to publish my book. This company was my last hope in every way.

Every single day, I wonder what my husband's life would have been like had he not married me; someone with a disease that they have no control over. Someone who is often looked down upon and someone who is often forced to question the validity of the condition they suffer from.

This dream I had would have made it possible for me never to have to question myself again. I know I could have helped people, and I know I could have helped myself.

I sit in my room every day and think. I look back on all of the people that were once in my life but aren't anymore. I think about all of the people that I once counted on. People that I would have done anything for, and I often did. Yes, there were times when I wasn't the perfect friend, but I was loyal to them, and I was there for them.

I don't know those people anymore. I have no family to reach out to. For a short time, I thought I might be able to rally some people together to help me, and when I tried, I was met with only a deafening silence.

My heart breaks for all the time I have lost in this life trying to be a better friend, the better sister, better aunt...better wife. I can't burden my dad with all of this, he has far too much to deal with already. I have my husband, and by God I am so grateful for that, but it's times like this that I would give anything to have a real, honest, I'll be right over friend.

Even a text message would help, or someone that could be broken-hearted and outraged, even if they were pretending just for me.

In a few weeks, I'm going to be 42. I never thought I would be so alone. I purposely sat down and tried to look into the future. What do I have on the horizon?

What can I look forward to? What can I plan for? Hope for? Nothing. I have no idea where I'm going, or what will happen next. At a time when I can barely get out of bed or stop crying for an hour at a time, I am once again questioning myself.

I was a fool for believing that I was good enough to make this happen. I won't even put the term "writer" on my profiles anymore. Being able to form a sentence, or tell a story doesn't make you an actual writer.

It's been a long time since I have been this low. In my future, all I see is more loss and heartache. One day, my dad. One day, our cats. None of them will be here forever. I'm alone except for my husband that I wish I hadn't dragged into this screwed up mess of a life.

It hurts. I am physically in as much pain as I am emotionally. The sad truth is, all I can imagine is people reading this, thinking "Oh boo hoo...get over it". Believe me, if it were an option I would get over it immediately, but it's not. Am I feeling sorry for myself? Yes, probably. Do I deserve to? Of course I do...and I don't give a shit if you don't agree.

If you can't be here for me during this time, then I don't need you in my life. I'm hurt, I'm angry, I'm heartbroken and devastated. I would expect that anyone that really cared could respect that. I wrote this book for me and only for me. To help get some of this off my chest so I don't have to carry it around with me. I'm sorry if you don't like it, but sometimes the truth hurts.

I have yet to determine whether I will keep writing after this. With each post, I always had my eye on the prize. This would be a book one day, and I would live my dream. Now I wonder if I was only experiencing delusions of grandeur.

I have put myself out there. Told my life story, and it was **rejected.** Do you have any idea what that feels like? I opened wounds that needed to stay closed in hopes that my story would make a difference. Perhaps, on a small scale it made some sort of difference, but on a larger scale?

Quite simply, I failed. Now I have to live with that.

48

THOUGHTS

There are days when the pain in your heart is so overwhelming that you can't think of anything else. With every breath, it feels as if your lungs are collapsing. I've been there and back so many times before. What could I do differently? How could I change this piece of the puzzle? It's such an odd experience when you feel so empty but so full of pain at the same time. The days are lonely.

The nights are hard. When you sleep, you never dream of anything but grief.

If actions speak louder than words, I'll have to scream at the top of my lungs. Words are all I have. For a very long time, I felt different inside. It seemed like I could conquer my fears. My only regret was the physical pain I had to endure, but I thought I was doing my best.

Every night, as I attempt to drift off to sleep, it hits me. I'm terrified. I am already so afraid of nothing and everything. Things that haven't even happened, things that might. I can't escape it.

I never thought I would be so very alone in life. I can no longer find the means to trust anyone. I've been running around with my heart on a silver platter for nearly 15 years, begging someone to take just enough to fill the void, leaving what I need to give to the man I love. Thank God for him, truly.

I hate myself that I can't just accept our life and our love as enough. I'm so grateful that he is in my life. It nearly kills me that I can't be the person that I need to be.

Thoughts keep running through my head. You'll regret this little breakdown when something bad really does happen. Regret, regret...regret. Why does it feel like I exist on the negative energy that word represents? It's so quiet here in this moment. Yet, all I can hear is noise. The tight feeling in my chest never seems to go away. I'm bored with this. Fed up with each and every emotion that grips me right now. Why couldn't it be something else?

I'm terrified of the future, and I can't forget the past. I feel stuck in the present, silently willing myself to move forward, but so afraid I can't. I'm trying to grow and learn from my life. But, I've studied this chapter a thousand times. It never changes. Don't you dare try to tell me that I have to change it. Do you know how often and how hard I've tried? Every single day is a struggle in this life. My head is cloudy. Words are jumbled together. Emotions are piled one on top of the other. Now nothing makes sense, and I can't make the connection.

Welcome to my Hell. Thank your lucky stars that you're just visiting.

EPILOGUE

Just to give you an idea of how unreliable bipolar disorder can be, my last post on June 17, 2015, was abysmal. Today, less than a month later I am grateful to say I am not in that place anymore. While it is true, a day may very well come where I am feeling that much pain, I am grateful to say that today, I am doing just fine. As you've made your way along the path of this journey with me, you've seen my highs and lows and everything in between. You've witness unbearable sadness, pain, grief, anger, and anxiety. However, at this point in my life, I am enjoying focusing on the good times in my life. I'm pushing aside all of the fears of what the future may bring, and learning to enjoy right now.

Looking out the window at this beautiful day, with music playing in my room and my amazing cat, Hayley lying on the bed next to me, I feel good. Summertime in Michigan always lifts my spirits. It seems like forever since June 2013 when I almost lost it all. I celebrated two years of being self-injury free last month, with the love of my life by my side. If that doesn't give me something to smile about, I don't know what would!

I have worked very hard to put 2013 behind me. Since then, many things have changed in my life. To start feeling better both mentally and physically, I eliminated Gluten from my diet. It has worked wonders for me. I know there are plenty of people of there that believe Gluten Sensitivity is all in your head, but these are the same people that would probably tell me to snap out of my depression. Needless to say, I set them and their opinions aside.

I have taken more steps to try to get physically healthy, and things are progressing. I still experience a great deal of pain, but even that has improved and I am seeking treatment as we speak.

One of the most important things that I have made sure to focus on is enjoying time with my husband. When we spend time together, I shut everything out and enjoy the moment. We have so much fun together, and we laugh more now than we did when we met 14 years ago. Joe and I have the best relationship and the greatest love for one another that I have ever witnessed. If someone were to ask me what I was proud of in my life, I would say my marriage. He is my world, and I love him more every single day. Of course, I can't forget my babies. We adopted a kitten from a shelter in December of 2013, and she is a handful. She adds so much color to our lives and completes our little family.

We've been fortunate enough to make some home improvements as well. One of the things that I love most in life is decorating. I'm often told that I am very good at it, and probably could have done it professionally. That makes me feel good. I put a lot of thought, time and energy into it.

After my last experience with a publishing company, as you have read, I was devastated. So beaten down that I was never again going to pursue this dream of becoming an author. I took several months off to heal. To find my voice again and get that old fire back. I am pleased to say I have found it. I am working with a fantastic company that treats me with respect, and I am so very grateful.

One of the most important things that has helped me change for the better is rediscovering my love of photography. My dad had some beautiful, professional cameras as I was growing up. He noticed my interest and eventually bought me one of my own. As I got older, I lost interest. I set my beautiful Minolta aside and asked for a good old point and shoot. I've used that type of camera for most of my life. I always remembered my first love and kept dreaming of the day when I could afford to buy myself a high-quality camera once again. I've been dropping hints to my husband for a few years, but it was just never possible financially.

This past year, for my birthday, my wish finally came true. I was given the incredible gift of a gorgeous Canon Rebel and just looking at it makes me smile. Joe was skeptical at first, but he always said that I was good at taking pictures, even with just a cell phone camera, so he gave in. Once he saw the beauty that you could create with a fantastic camera, he was sold. We both continue to marvel at the gorgeous pictures I can take. I am enjoying taking courses online in photography, and sharing what I learn with my friends and family.

Yes, life is much, much better. The bad times do come, but they don't seem to last as long. The sadness overwhelms me, but most days I can find a way to channel it into something positive. I know now that feeling sad doesn't make it a bad life, just a bad day. I had to leave a lot of people behind in the course of finding myself again. However, I also forged new bonds. I know that if times are hard, I do have people in my life I can go to.

As far as treatment, at this time in my life, I have chosen to get medication refills from my primary care physician. I feel as if he is one of the very few doctors in my life I can trust. This step is not right for everyone, and I do not advise taking that decision lightly.

We have an understanding that should things take a drastic turn, I will look for someone in the mental health field.

There's just one more thing. I've always scoffed at the people in this world that believe being positive can change your life. What a ridiculous notion, right? I decided one day to try it. I challenged myself to go on social media every day and select two people that I would contact with a positive message. The response was overwhelming. When you make others feel good, even about something simple, it does come back to you. Does this mean I am no longer Bipolar? Oh, hell no! But I'll be damned if it doesn't make some of the crap life throws at you just seem inconsequential.

Am I cured? Sadly, no. Will I go through hard times again? Sadly, yes. At least this time around, I'm much more self-aware. Perhaps that comes with age and experience, maybe it comes from a series of choices that you make, or it could be just pure dumb luck. Regardless, I know that telling my story has been one of the best decisions I could have made for myself.

I want to thank everyone that has helped me through my worst days and smiled right alongside me during my best days. You know who you are, and you know that I love you. By letting me into your life, despite all the baggage that I bring, you have gained a powerful friend and ally.

REBECCA'S STORY IN THE MEDIA!

On November 26th, 2014, Rebecca joined Lori Faitel and Tonia Wittkower on their show titled "The Science of Happiness." The show is a weekly feature on Brain Injury Radio, a station with over 1,000 episodes, helping to inform and provide a platform for traumatic brain injury survivors. In the interview, Rebecca discussed how depression, specifically bipolar disorder, can affect a person's daily life, something many brain injury survivors struggle with everyday.

Here is a peek into the informative interview. Hear the full episode on Blog Talk Radio, and visit BrainInjuryRadio.com to learn more about the mission to help those struggling with traumatic brain injury, mental health related issues, and more.

****

Lori: I'd like you to feel free to go ahead and explain to people who you are beyond what I said. The mic is yours.

Rebecca: I started feeling as if something wasn't quite wired right in my brain when I was in the senior year of high school, and I could feel that some days I just didn't want to talk to anybody, I didn't want to be around anybody, but maybe a few hours later I'd be bouncing off the walls, telling jokes, and, you know, I was the life of the party. And then eventually I would experience the suicidal thoughts where I'd spend all of my time in my room listening to the same songs over and over and over again. Finally when I was 19, I went to my parents and said, "I think something's wrong" because I'm taking 10 plus Excedrin PMs to go to sleep at night and then taking No-doze to stay awake all day, so I said "We gotta talk to somebody." I was 19 when I was diagnosed and put on medication, and I'm 41 now, so as you can imagine I've spent a lot of years of ups-and-downs, and a lot to deal with. Thankfully, I met my husband. We met officially in 1999, we married in 2001, and he's been a constant supporter for me. He's always there. He understands what I'm going through. We've been married for 13 years now, and he can sense it now almost as much as I can. You get to a point in your life where you'd like to believe that you could figure out what's going on with you, and what you can expect, and know how to fix it. You never do because bipolar disorder lies to you. It tells you you're not worth it, not good enough, and you believe it because you feel so completely miserable. Then the mania will be very brief. Suddenly, you feel like you can take on the world. Then the next day you feel like you can't even get out of bed. So, it [bipolar disorder] is a very deceptive disease, very painful. You feel things deeper than anyone else does. It's not to say other people don't experience the same type of pain, but even a small injury or a small heartache, you feel it ten times deeper.

Last year, I went through a very difficult time and I did try to take my own life. I was hospitalized in a horrible, horrible hospital. When I came out, I started to write. Writing is something I wanted to do since I was in the third grade. But, once you get depressed, you can't really find it in yourself to get your thoughts together most of the time. I started to write a blog. I published it, and eventually people were coming to me saying "Thank you. Now I understand. I was able to talk to my husband or my spouse, about what's going on with me. Now I'm getting help." I heard from people frequently, and I thought that maybe I can take this negative, horrible thing that has happened to me and turn it into a positive by starting to try to help people, instead of sitting around and wishing I was doing better.

Ironically, today is my mom's birthday. She passed away in 2008, and I just wanted to say something about her because my goal, ever since she's been gone, has been to make her proud. One day I plan on doing that.

Knowing What Helps You

Beth: What is it that helps you the most? How do you work with your hidden disability?

Rebecca: What helps me the most, this may sound cheesy, but the thing that helps me the most is my husband. He keeps me level when there isn't anything else in the world that could possibly keep me level. He knows how to make me smile when I have no desire to smile. I have a lot of things I enjoy like reading, a lot of movies, a lot of sports, and things like that. I actually do pet sit on the side. We have cats of our own. Caring for animals helps me. And, writing. Writing is a huge thing for me. I write my blog as often as I can. When I've written and left everything on the page, it's almost like a weight has been lifted off of my shoulders because it's there, it's not on me anymore. It helps a lot because for 20 straight years I couldn't write one word. Suddenly, it came back to me and it now helps. I strongly suggest, even if it doesn't make sense, writing words or sentences saying *I feel like this today*. It can really help you out a lot.

Getting Involved and Being a Lantern of Hope

Lori: Did you chat or go back and forth with people on your blog? Do people leave you messages?

Rebecca: Yes, almost weekly I'm getting messages from people. They do a lot of advertising for the blog on Twitter, and I get a lot of responses back on Twitter as well. I reach out to all of them and say "Hey, if you need to talk any further, you can reach me here." I've had people from Malaysia tell me that now they can explain to their family or to their husband what exactly is wrong with them and that they no longer feel alone. It's incredible to me that I have that much reach.

On triggers and outside noise

Beth: Sometimes there is too much stimulation, too much noise, too much this or too much that, and it can bring on the depression. It can throw me into a tailspin. Sometimes I fear of things I can't do and then I just shut down. I don't know how that might relate to bipolar [disorder], is there stimulations there?

Rebecca: Yes, it's very similar. When you're in a situation where there's just too much outside noise, it can launch you straight into a panic attack. One of the reasons is because I spent so many years dealing with agoraphobia, which is essentially the fear of open spaces. If I go anywhere it's with my husband, because he can tell when I'm getting uncomfortable and he can help me navigate the situation or get me out of the situation. And yes, if there is too much outside interference, too many things going on, or someone expects too much out of me at that moment; I will also just completely shut down. There's nothing I can really do to fix it at that moment. I just have to go away, or I have to be alone. I have to work through it in my own way and there are a lot of people that just do not understand that.

On losing friends

Beth: When you found yourself in a situation like that, did your friends fall away from you?

Rebecca: Yes. Absolutely 100%. Last summer, I can't even count the number of people that left my life, including family members, especially with something like a suicide attempt. There are many people who feel like anyone who tries that is just selfish and only cares about themselves. I always like to say, when someone tells me how selfish I am, that I have this image of myself sitting in the corner of the room hogging all the depression to myself because I'm so selfish. People don't understand that it's not selfish, it's because you can't overcome the amount of pain you're in and you feel as if you being here is causing more pain than if you weren't here. Eventually you learn that that's not the case, but at that moment, that's all you can think of.

I had people that were in my life for 20 years or more that just dropped off the face of the Earth and could just not speak to me, deleted me on Facebook. I have kind of a lonely life now that I'm rebuilding and learning how to trust people again, because so many people backed away. Even family members, which is very, very painful.

Beth: When you think that people will reach out and draw you closer to protect you, they fall away. My heart breaks when I hear that.

Rebecca: It's a very hard situation. I understand that of course if they're experiencing some kind of pain because they think of me as being gone, I can completely understand that. But once I made it, and I survived it, and they still just couldn't be around me or talk to me or tolerate me, I felt like they were no longer necessary in my life anymore. You really have to learn the difference between people that are true friends and who are not, especially in these types of situations.

On Downward Spirals

Lori: As a traumatic brain injury survivor, I went through a few months when I had no confidence, I thought that everything I did was wrong, I thought that nobody liked me, even when my mom would call me and tell me she loved me, I thought for sure she was just saying that because she had to. I would just lay in my bed and cry, and that didn't help anything. It would give me a headache, things were just terrible. Is that something like the depression you go through?

Rebecca: Very much so. The smallest things can trigger it. Your brother had asked me if I had any specific triggers I watch out for. I know I haven't touched on this too much, because it is kind of a sensitive subject as someone recovering from self-injury. Self-injury is a very, very dangerous thing. I found that outside sources will trigger me to want to do that. I think that certain people in my life will trigger me. Even getting up in the morning sometimes is a trigger for me. I know it sounds crazy, but it's true. If I get up in the morning and the night before I've made myself a 12-page list of everything I feel I need to get done, and I can't get any of that done, I will automatically crash. I set too high of expectations of myself, I have to learn to just get up and say *Okay, you're awake now, in a little while why don't you try this.* Learn self-talk is very, very important. Talk to yourself. Tell yourself, *this is okay for right now. Let's try this in a little while.*

Going into a downward spiral — sometimes I have no control over it and I have no reason for it. I'll wake up one morning and feel like there's a weight on my back, and I can't fix it. My husband can't fix it. That's the hardest part for him, because as a loved one, we don't want to see our spouse in pain. We want to help, and when we can't, it gets frustrating. And, that's a dynamic you just have to face. One person is frustrated because they can't get help and the other person's frustrated because they can't understand. The work to get yourself out of one of those spirals is so exhausting and people just don't get it. All I can say is that it's the hardest thing in the world. Every time I do it and I come out okay, is another time when I call myself a survivor.

Rebecca Lombardo

ACKNOWLEDGEMENTS

I have many people that I am grateful to have in my life. Especially those that hung on when I was pretty sure I was going to let go. Even if you may have been absent during my struggles, chances are pretty good that you made a difference in my life in one way or another, and for that I am so thankful.

To my Mom.
There are not enough words in the world to describe how much I love and miss you. All I ever wanted was to make you proud, and I sincerely hope I have done that. You were not only my mom but my best friend.

To my brother, Dana.
Since you've been gone, I have often felt a profound sense of loss. We may not have always agreed on everything, but the things we did share are special to me, and I continue to think of you every day.

To my sister, Karen.
I will always cherish the fond memories I have of the times we shared. We laughed a lot and had a lot of fun. We may have grown apart over the years, but I will always be able to look back on the good times. Thank you.

To my brother, Rick.
When I was just a little kid, you took me under your wing and became one of my best friends. I'll never forget driving up to 7-11 in your white Mustang. You were there for me, and I will always be grateful.

To my brother, Jeff.

I spent a lot of my life looking up to you. You are so smart, funny and gifted. If we never mend our relationship completely, please know that when I look back on our story, I always try remember the good times. The inside jokes and the laughter we shared will forever hold a special place in my heart.

To my brother, Brad.

Out of all of the members of my family, you are the one I am most similar to. You were a non-stop source of laughter in our lives. I still look back and smile as I recall some of the jokes we shared. I have missed you constantly since you moved away. You have been there for me through some hard times, and you will never know how grateful I am. I love you.

To my niece, Katie.

When you were a kid, I loved spending time with you, curling your hair and trying to teach you French. As the years have gone by, we have grown into two very different people, and that's OK. I just want you to be happy. I will always look back and smile at the times we've shared.

To Emily, Nolan, and Lance.

I love you all so much. I know we don't get to spend much time together these days, but please know that I hold a very special place for you in my heart. You are all so amazing, smart and beautiful. I wish you all nothing but happiness and success. Aunt Beka is always here for you.

To my Dad.

You have and always will be my hero. You slaved and sacrificed to raise us, and I am eternally grateful to you. You helped shape me into the person I am today. Every day, I catch myself becoming more like you. No matter what life brings, you and Mom have always been my light in the storm. I will always cherish the times we have spent together. I love you now and forever.

To my husband, Joe.

It's hard for me to look back on some of the things I have put you through in the last 14 years. It breaks my heart to know that there were times when you were afraid of what the future may bring because of my illness. I cry happy tears when I think of all of the time you were there to catch me when I fell. You are my world. Without you, I would not be sitting here writing this. I will never be able to express the gratitude I feel for your patience with me. I have never loved someone as much as I love you. You are what kept me going when all I wanted was to give up. Forever will never be enough time to spend with you. Thank you to your Mom, and your whole family for caring, understanding and being supportive. We are all so proud of you and the man you have become. Your Dad, Grandma and Uncle Johnny are smiling down on you with pride. I only hope that I can make you as happy as you have made me. I love you.

To my Facebook Family.

Thank you doesn't seem like enough. Every one of you has been there for me, in one way or another. We may not always get to see each other in person, but just knowing you are out there, I don't feel quite so alone. You are amazing people, and I love you all.

CONNECT WITH REBECCA

Want to continue the journey with Rebecca?
Subscribe to her internationally followed blog at
Judgmentfreezone2013.blogspot.com.

Follow Rebecca on Twitter at @BekaLombardo
and like the official It's Not Your Journey" Facebook
page at Facebook.com/notyourjourney

Or visit her official website at:
www.rebeccalombardo.com